THE PATRIARCHAL AGE

Other books by Charles F. Pfeiffer

BAKER'S BIBLE ATLAS

BETWEEN THE TESTAMENTS

THE DEAD SEA SCROLLS

THE BOOK OF GENESIS

THE BOOK OF LEVITICUS

THE PATRIARCHAL AGE

Charles F. Pfeiffer

BAKER BOOK HOUSE
Grand Rapids 6, Michigan
1961

Library of Congress Catalog Card Number: 61-12008
First printed, May 1961

PHOTOLITHOPRINTED BY CUSHING - MALLOY, INC.
ANN ARBOR, MICHIGAN, UNITED STATES OF AMERICA
1961

CONTENTS

Preface 9
1. The Biblical Patriarchs: History or Fancy? 11
2. Patriarchal Organization 15
3. Men and Tribes 19
4. The Patriarchs: Abraham, Isaac, Jacob 23
5. The Peoples Among Whom the Patriarchs Lived 29
6. The Cities of the Patriarchs 43
7. Canaan During Patriarchal Times 49
8. An Episode in World Politics 57
9. The Religion of the Canaanites 61
10. The Daily Lives of the Patriarchs 71
11. Social and Business Life in Patriarchal Times 77
12. The God Whom the Patriarchs Worshiped 85
13. The Patriarchal Institutions 89
14. The Theology of the Patriarchs 97
15. The Patriarchs and Divine Revelation 103
16. Law in Patriarchal Times 107
17. The Literature of the Patriarchal Age 117
Bibliography 120

PREFACE

When the Lord identified Himself to Moses from the burning bush, He said, "I am . . . the God of Abraham, the God of Isaac, and the God of Jacob" (Exod. 3:6). Although the experience of the Exodus and the precepts of the Mosaic Law were focal points of later prophetic thought, the earlier events in the lives of the patriarchs served as a continuing challenge throughout the history of Israel – as they continue to do today.

Genesis is the "Book of Beginnings," and it gives considerable attention to the beginnings of Israel. The tribal organization is traced to the twelve sons of Jacob-Israel. He, in turn, is described as the son of Isaac, and the grandson of Abraham. It was divine election which had called Abraham from Ur of the Chaldees, and which subsequently chose Isaac instead of Ishmael, and Jacob instead of Esau. The patriarchal records are interesting as literature, but the inspired author clearly wanted us to be more than entertained. He saw in the history of the patriarchs the accomplishment of divine purposes. Man might lie and cheat – and suffer the consequences of sin – but God was ever in the shadows "keeping watch above His own."

In brief compass the present study seeks to examine the faith and institutions of the Patriarchal Age. Some attention has been given to the political and religious life of the world in which they moved. Although archaeological discoveries contain no explicit reference to the patriarchs, they yield much material on the life of the people who were contemporary with the patriarchs.

No attempt has been made to work out an exact chronology for the period. For practical purposes the present volume covers the period between 2000 and 1500 B.C., except that it discusses the history of Israel only as far as the settlement of Jacob and his sons in Egypt.

The essential historicity of the Biblical record and the essential reliability of the Biblical text are presuppositions in the present study. This does not preclude the recognition of epic features in the narrative; but it does presume that the Biblical writers sought to communicate a body of factual material which, with due regard to form and style, can be objectively studied.

It is the hope of the author to introduce many whose sole knowledge of the Patriarchal Age comes from Scripture, to the wealth of extra-Biblical material which makes it possible to see the sacred text in its wider context.

Charles F. Pfeiffer

Beverly Farms, Mass.
March 18, 1961

THE
PATRIARCHAL
AGE

1

THE BIBLICAL PATRIARCHS: HISTORY OR FANCY?

Biblical scholars have frequently been skeptical concerning the existence of the men who are presented in Scripture as the physical and spiritual progenitors of Israel and, in a wider sense, the spiritual fathers of all who trust the God of Israel, and his Son, Jesus Christ. It has become accepted procedure to begin the history of Israel with the Exodus from Egypt, and to make a few allusions to the patriarchs in an introduction or preface.[1]

William F. Albright, who has a high respect for the historicity of the patriarchs, has written, "Until recently it was the fashion among biblical historians to treat the patriarchal sagas of Genesis as though they were artificial creations of Israelite scribes of the Divided Monarchy or tales told by imaginative rhapsodists around Israelite campfires during the centuries following their occupation of the country."[2] It was thought that varying traditions, representing the different ethnic groups which formed the nation of Israel had been fused into one continuous narrative. It has been suggested, for example, that an "Abraham tradition" existed at the cult center of Hebron, and that an "Isaac tradition" had its center at Beer-sheba. A fusion of the two took place, and Isaac was regarded as the son of Abraham.

In the writings of G. A. Danell,[3] we are told that Abraham, the cult-hero of the Hebron region, was taken over by the nation of Israel at the time of the monarchy. The same ideas are propounded in the writings of J. Pedersen[4] of Copenhagen, who suggested that the stories of the patriarchs had a utilitarian pur-

1. e.g. Martin Noth, *The History of Israel* and Bernhard W. Anderson, *Understanding the Old Testament.*
2. W. F. Albright, "The Biblical Period," in *The Jews: Their History, Culture, and Religion,* edited by Louis Finkelstein.
3. G. A. Danell, *Studies in the Namc Israel in the Old Testament,* pp. 34-35.
4. J. Pedersen, *Israel, III-IV,* pp. 666-669.

pose: "to prove the right of Israel to Canaan." Pedersen observes that "no one disputed this right in pre-exilic times," and therefore gives an intolerably late date to the patriarchal narratives. His conclusion was that "all the main features of the stories about Abraham are coloured by the time after the regal period."

This attitude is basically that of the nineteenth century Old Testament scholar whose famous *Prolegomena to the History of Israel* marked a landmark in Biblical scholarship. Living before the day of archaeological discovery, Wellhausen could write in all good conscience, "We attain to no historical knowledge of the patriarchs, but only of the time when the stories about them arose in the Israelite people; this latter age is here unconsciously projected, in its inner and its outward features, into hoary antiquity, and is reflected there like a glorified image."[5]

Although Wellhausen is still respected for his contribution to Biblical studies, his modern disciples have had to modify many of his conclusions. Archaeological discoveries during the past half century show us that the patriarchal narratives fit in the period in which the Bible places them, and in no other. The clay tablets from Nuzi and Mari have helped us to visualize the political and the social world in which the patriarchs moved. The conjectures of Wellhausen made sense in the years before the discovery of vast quantities of literature from a period contemporary with the patriarchs. We are less dependent on hypothetical reconstructions of history now that we have actual historical records.

It should not be assumed, however, that current Old Testament scholarship has reverted to a "pre-critical" attitude toward the patriarchal narratives (Gen. 12-50). Albright speaks of the "substantial historicity of patriarchal tradition," although he does not insist on accuracy in detail.

A contemporary writer in the field of Biblical Theology, Gerhard Von Rad, rejects the higher critical principles associated with Wellhausen. In their place he studies the "units" of narration, a procedure known as "Form Criticism" which is applied to both Old Testament and New Testament studies. Von Rad and the form critics consider that each story in the Biblical text forms a "unit" which had a separate history of its own.[6] In the process of time individual units were incorporated into great

5. Julius Wellhausen, *Prolegomena to the History of Israel,* (English Translation) pp. 318-319.
6. Gerhard Von Rad, *Theologie des Alten Testaments,* Band I, p. 7 ff.

blocks of traditional material. As the final stage of the process these "blocks" were incorporated into the books of our Bible.

The results of Form Criticism may become quite arbitrary, however. John Bright in his recent book, *A History of Israel,*[7] sounds a warning against the results which may be expected from Form Criticism: "To pick and choose from the traditions . . . according historicity to this, while denying it to that, is a most subjective procedure, reflecting no more than one's own predelections. Nor is there any objective method by which the history of the traditions may be traced, and historical worth assayed by examination of the traditions themselves. Form Criticism, indispensable as it is in understanding and interpreting the traditions cannot, in the nature of the case, pass judgment on historicity in the absence of external evidence."

Aside from the Scriptures themselves, the only objective way of testing the historicity of the patriarchal records is to examine them in the light of the facts which archaeology has made available to us. We will have to admit that the patriarchs themselves are not mentioned in any non-Biblical document, but we have no reason to believe they should be so mentioned. Abraham, Isaac, and Jacob, according to Scripture dwelt "in tents," having separated themselves from the centers of urban life. If we can find non-Biblical texts which describe the kind of life presented in the Biblical account of Genesis 12-50 (which varies in a marked degree from the situation after the tribes entered Canaan under Joshua), we have at least presumptive evidence that the Biblical text reflects genuine history.

The verdict of Albright, quoted above, is that archaeology has provided such materials. In the Introductory Volume to *The Interpreter's Bible,* James Muilenberg wrote, "Archaeology has revealed an extraordinary correspondence between the general social and cultural conditions portrayed in Genesis and those exposed by excavations. Discoveries from such sites as Nuzi, Mari, and elsewhere, provide the geographical, cultural, linguistic, and religious background against which the stories of the patriarchs are laid."[8]

Although the tendency of modern Biblical scholarship has been to have a higher regard for the historicity of the patriarchal records than that held by many writers a generation or two ago, the theological use of that fact varies considerably. The con-

7. John Bright, *A History of Israel,* p. 69.
8. James Muilenburg, "The History of the Religion of Israel," *Interpreter's Bible,* I, p. 296.

servative may feel that his doctrine of verbal inspiration has been made intellectually respectable because the views of the Wellhausen school have been so rudely upset. The liberal, however, will see the similarity between religious institutions of ancient Israel and her neighbors of the Fertile Crescent as a reason for denying any uniqueness to the faith of the Old Testament. The neo-orthodox will be content with the "essential" historicity of the Biblical records and stress the importance of a personal divine encounter as embodying the true "word of God." In a very real sense theologians interpret the facts of archaeology, as they do the facts of Scripture, in accord with their basic presuppositions. Aside, however, from the overtones which may be read into the facts, we can now assert without fear of contradiction that the Biblical patriarchs need not be regarded as demigods or characters from the realm of folk-lore. They appear as real men, living in a real world which is now well-known because of the work of modern archaeology.

2

PATRIARCHAL ORGANIZATION

The term "patriarch" is expressive of the social structure under which the earliest Israelites lived. The father was recognized as both legal and spiritual head of the family. Wives and children were dependent upon the father, or patriarch, of the family, who also served as its governor, priest, and magistrate. The family, including its slaves, was subject to the patriarch, who represented the sole authority, under God.

It was the absence of any constituted government that caused the patriarch to rule without external restraint. As the head of the family, the patriarch assumed responsibility for its welfare. When Joseph, in Egypt, sent word through Reuben that Benjamin should be sent to Egypt, aged Jacob was understandably concerned. In anguish he exclaimed, "You have bereaved me of my children: Joseph is no more and Simeon is no more, and now ye would take Benjamin . . . " (Gen. 42:36) . Thereupon Reuben, the eldest of the brothers and their spokesman, stated, "Slay my two sons if I do not bring him back to you" (Gen. 42:37) . This offer was in accord with principles which we meet in the Code of Hammurabi. There we read that a man who causes the death of another's daughter is made to suffer by having his own daughter slain. It was a matter of the rights of one father against the rights of another father.

The patriarchal records in the Bible presuppose the absolute power of a father over the very lives of his children. The record of Abraham's preparation to offer Isaac on Mount Moriah (Gen. 22) emphasizes the feelings of the father and his obedience to God. The thought that Isaac should have been consulted is foreign to the spirit of the record. Abraham, as the patriarch, had full control over the life of his son. When Jacob, under pressure of famine, decided to send Benjamin to Egypt, the patriarch alone made the decision: "Take also your brother," he said to his older sons with the observation, "If I am bereaved of my children, I am bereaved" (Gen. 43:13-14). Both Abraham and Jacob dearly loved their children. Their welfare was a major concern, but the concern was in terms of a patriarchal type of society.

Similar control was exercised by the patriarchs over their daughters. Lot was embarrassed when the men of Sodom wanted to have homosexual relations with two "men" to whom he had accorded the hospitality of his home. Rather than breach the laws of hospitality, which guaranteed protection to the visitor while under one's roof, Lot said to the men of Sodom, "Behold, I have two daughters who have not known man; let me bring them out to you and do to them as you please, only do nothing to these men, for they have come under the shelter of my roof" (Gen. 19-8). Lot's sense of the demands of hospitality caused him to offer to sacrifice his daughters to mob violence. As patriarch of his family, Lot considered that he had the right to dispose of the girls as he wished.

Emphasis on patriarchal authority might produce situations which would seem to us inhuman. The Biblical records make it clear, however, that true love existed among the members of patriarchal family groups. Abraham's love for Ishmael (Gen. 17:18), and subsequently for Isaac (Gen. 22:2), form an important factor in the life of the patriarch. The love, however, was always expressed within the framework of patriarchal life.

The patriarch of the family, or tribe, had not only the right of absolute control, but also the duty to punish those guilty of crime. When Laban pursued Jacob, complaining because of the theft of the *teraphim,* or household gods, Jacob protested innocence, and added: "Any one with whom you find your gods shall not live" (Gen. 31:32). It was Jacob's duty, as head of the household, to enforce principles of right-doing.

The family unit included not only the father, his wives and their children, but also the sons and their wives. Levirate marriage customs brought the wives into a permanent relationship with the family of their husbands. When Judah learned that Tamar, his widowed daughter-in-law, was pregnant, he demanded, "Bring her out and let her be burned" (Gen. 38:24). Tamar had been married, successively, to two sons of Judah, and she was expected to await the third. When Judah withheld his third son, Tamar disguised herself as a prostitute in order to entice Judah, himself, to father a child. In demanding the death of a daughter-in-law who had violated the laws of chastity, Judah was within his rights. In this instance, however, Tamar was spared in view of the fact that the patriarch himself was equally guilty.

Concepts of patriarchal authority are reflected in the Mosaic Law. Not only do we read, "Honor your father and your mother that your days may be long in the land which the Lord your God gives you" (Exod. 20:12) but we also read of the punishment meted out to the one who shows contempt for his parents: "Whoever strikes his father or his mother shall be put to death" (Exod. 21:15); "Whoever curses his father or his mother shall be put to death" (Exod. 21:17).

A procedure is outlined for the treatment of a rebellious son: "If a man has a stubborn and rebellious son, who will not obey the voice of his father or the voice of his mother, and, though they chastise him, will not give heed to them, then his father and his mother shall take hold of him, and bring him out to the elders of his city at the gate of the place where he lives, and they shall say to the elders of his city, 'This our son is stubborn and rebellious, he will not obey our voice; he is a glutton and a drunkard.' Then all the men of the city shall stone him to death with stones; so they shall purge the evil from your midst; and all Israel shall hear, and fear" (Deut. 21:18-21).

The patriarch maintained his position throughout life, being succeeded, normally, by his eldest son. Another successor might be chosen, however. Jacob set aside the principle of primogeniture when he called Reuben "unstable as water," and said to him, "You shall not have the pre-eminence" (Gen. 49:4). Judah was designated as the one who would bear the scepter over the sons of Jacob (Israel) (Gen. 49:8-12).

In the course of a few generations, the patriarchal family would grow unwieldy. Instead of a family, it should then be called a clan, and it would often be wise for it to break up into smaller units. We read that Esau "went into a land away from his brother Jacob, for their possessions were too great for them to dwell together" (Gen. 35:6-7). Judah appears to have started a separate family when he "went down from his brothers" (Gen. 38:1) and married a Canaanite girl. A number of clans with common ties of family and tradition might function together as a tribe.

The social structure of family (sometimes called "father's house"), clan, and tribe finds its fullest expression in Scripture during the period following the Exodus. Gideon, we are told, was a member of a family in the clan of Abiezer (Judg. 6:11) of the tribe of Manasseh. When called to lead Israel against the Midianite oppressors, he objected: "Behold, my clan is the weakest in Manasseh, and I am the least in my family" (Judg. 6:15).

In a patriarchal society with no external authority, some means must be found to insure law and order among various tribal groups. The most basic of these among the ancient Semitic peoples was the concept of blood revenge. Murder was regarded as a tribal matter, and the family of a slain man sought vengeance on the murderer or his tribe. It was considered a tribal obligation for members of a tribe to avenge the wrong done to one of their fellows.

3

MEN AND TRIBES

It has often been suggested that the descriptions of the Biblical patriarchs are actually records of the movements and activities of whole tribes. Terms such as "son" and "beget" may be used metaphorically, and in some instances the Biblical writers use them to show the relationships of ethnic groups. When, for instance, we read that Canaan became the father of Sidon, his firstborn (Gen. 10:15) we understand that the city of Sidon was the first of the great Canaanite cities, although later surpassed by Tyre. That the author of Genesis was thinking of Sidon as a city is clear, for he continues, "and the territory of the Canaanites extended from Sidon, in the direction of Gerar, as far as Gaza" (10:19). We also read in Genesis 10 that Canaan was the father of "the Jebusites, the Amorites, the Girgashites, the Hivites, the Arkites, the Sinites, the Arvadites, the Zemarites, and the Hamathites" (Gen. 10:16-18) – all ethnic groups or city-states of Canaan. Among the descendants of Keturah, Abraham's second wife, we find Midian and Shuah (Gen. 25:1), both of whom appear later as tribes (cf. Exod.2:15; Job 2:11). Genealogical tables often are used to show relationships among peoples. Those who compiled them did not hesitate to omit generations when it suited their purpose to do so and, on occasion, to use tribal designations.

In the records of the patriarchs themselves, however, there is no hint that we are dealing with large tribal groups. We may explain the mobility of Abraham in terms of ethnic movements during the early second millennium B.C., but the Scripture makes it clear that the particular movement of which we are reading is that of the man Abraham. This is evident in the care that is taken to insure that the sons of the patriarchs will marry the right type of girls. Great effort was expended to send back to Paddan-aram in order to secure a bride for

Isaac. Abraham received specific promises which were to be fulfilled in his son.

We must recognize, however, that the movements of Abraham and his household do involve more than a few people. The covenant promise was limited to a blood relationship, but the larger "household" of the patriarch was such that he could muster three hundred and eighteen trained men to rescue his nephew Lot (Gen. 14:14). The rite of circumcision was performed on the entire household: "he that is born in your house and he that is bought with your money" (Gen. 17:13).

In spite of the efforts of the patriarchs to keep their line free from the corrupting influences of paganism, an early breakdown in family distinctiveness is carefully recorded in Scripture. Isaac and Rebekah were grieved because Esau married Hittite girls (Gen. 26:34-35). Although Jacob married wives from Paddan-aram, his son Judah married a Canaanite (Gen. 38:2). Joseph, in Egypt, was married to the daughter of Potiphera, the priest of On (Gen. 41:45), and Moses, while in the wilderness, married the daughter of a Midianite priest (Exod. 2:15-22).

The Israelites, like other peoples of both ancient and modern times, developed a heterogeneous society and culture. We read of Hobab in the wilderness (Num. 10:29-32): Rahab at Jericho (Judg. 6:25), the Gibeonites (Josh. 9); and Ruth the Moabitess being incorporated into the people of Israel. Many of these people could claim no blood relationship with Abraham, but they shared his faith and entered into the promises which God had given him. The patriarchs were men. They gave birth to tribes which soon incorporated varying ethnic elements

The name Israel, rather than Abraham, is the term used to describe those who trace their history back to the patriarch who first entered Canaan. Israel is presented to us in Scripture as an alternate name for Jacob. The concept of Israel the man is merged into that of Israel the nation in Genesis 46:3-4. Jacob had learned that his son Joseph was alive and prospering in Egypt. The aged father had reached Beer-sheba, but he was still hesitant about moving farther. God spoke to him, however, in a theophany, saying, "I am God, the God of your father; do not be afraid to go down to Egypt; for I will there make of you a great nation. I will go down with you to Egypt, and I will also bring you up again; and Joseph's hand shall close your eyes." Here the man Jacob was told that he would die in Egypt — his son Joseph would close his eyes in death. The nation Jacob-Israel, would become great in Egypt, and God would bring them back into Canaan. This fact is given to Jacob as a means of assurance. His concern would not be with his own future life. As a mortal he would go "the way of all the earth" (cf. I Kings 2:2), but he could feel that his life had not been wasted, his posterity would be multiplied and brought back to the land which God had promised to Abraham.

4

THE PATRIARCHS: ABRAHAM, ISAAC, JACOB

The lives of the patriarchs are depicted in realistic terms. They were men of faith, but not always faithful men. Yet Scripture does emphasize the sovereignty of God in their lives. Abraham lied concerning the identity of Sarah, and Jacob cheated his brother and deceived his father. In each instance, however, God used the hour of spiritual defeat to impart lessons which would result in growth in grace.

It is with good reason that Abraham is esteemed the father of the faithful of all ages (Gal. 3:7). In the great "faith chapter" we read, "By faith Abraham obeyed when he was called to go out to a place which he was to receive as an inheritance; and he went out, not knowing where he was to go" (Heb. 11:8). Believing God, Abraham left Ur together with his father (Gen. 11:31; Acts 7:1-4); then left Haran and went toward Canaan, a land both unknown to him and lacking in the high civilization of the Mesopotamian cities which were left behind.

Abraham was a man of "like passions" with ourselves, however. He seems to have delayed in Haran when he should have moved on into Canaan (Gen. 11:31 – 12:5). His decision to go to Egypt for food in a time of famine need not be interpreted as a lack of faith (Gen. 12:10), but his conduct there certainly was unbecoming a child of God (Gen. 12:11-16). Abraham decided to lie, or tell a half truth (which is just as bad), in order to protect himself from Pharaoh. By stating that Sarah was his sister, Abraham placed her in a compromising position, and Pharaoh had no hesitancy in taking her for his harem (Gen. 12:15). It is true that Abraham expected to be honored as Sarah's brother, whereas he might have been killed as her husband (Gen. 12:12, 16). Nevertheless the action was contrary to human decency as well as the demand for truthfulness on the part of those who bear the name of God. Pharaoh learned the truth, and Abraham was ushered out of Egypt in disgrace (cf. Gen. 12:17-20).

Abraham's impatience in awaiting an heir is understandable, but it also indicated a lack of faith. The expedience of having a child by Hagar, Sarah's maid, was in accord with the customs of the day, but it was contrary to the purpose of God (Gen. 16:2; 17:19). In due time a son was born to Sarah, and Abraham's plans for Ishmael had to be seriously altered.

The lapses of Abraham, however, do not eclipse his greatness. It took both courage and faith to leave the comforts of Ur and embark on a spiritual pilgrimage. Suffering through a famine in a strange land was, itself, a sore trial. The greatheartedness of Abraham was never more manifest than in his dealings with Lot. The very fact that differences should arise between the herdsmen of the two men reminds us of the conflict of interests inherent in all human relationships. Age and position would have justified Abraham in deciding matters unilaterally. Instead, however, he gave Lot his choice of the land (Gen. 13:8-13), whereupon the Lord renewed the promise that Canaan would one day be the inheritance of Abraham's descendants (Gen. 13:14-17).

The supreme test of Abraham came, however, after his son Isaac had reached maturity. God had said that Isaac would be the heir to the promises given to Abraham. Now all this appeared to be canceled. God gave the strange command to take the lad to the mountains of Moriah and there offer him as a sacrifice (Gen. 22:1-2). There is no hint of hesitancy in the actions of the patriarch. He went, with the full assurance of faith that "God was able to raise men even from the dead" (Heb. 11:19). And God did intervene. A ram was offered instead of Isaac, for Abraham had proved himself worthy of the title, Father of the Faithful.

The apostle Paul consistently regarded Abraham as the supreme example of faith: "He staggered not at the promise of God through unbelief; but was strong in faith, giving glory to God; and being fully persuaded that, what he had promised, he was able also to perform. And therefore, it was imputed to him for righteousness" (Rom. 4:20-22). James showed that the faith of Abraham was manifest in his works: "You see that faith was active along with his works, and faith was completed by works" (James 2:22).

Isaac's life is largely associated with that of his father, Abraham, and his son, Jacob. The twin sons of Isaac and Rebekah differed in temperament. Esau was an outdoor man who particularly pleased Isaac, but Jacob stayed closer to home and became the darling of Rebekah.

Obedient in not going down to Egypt (Gen. 26:2), Isaac nevertheless followed the pattern of Abraham in lying about his wife to Abimelech, king of the Philistine state of Gerar. Much of Isaac's life was spent in southern Canaan in the vicinity of Gerar, Rehoboth, and Beer-sheba.

The rivalry between Jacob and Esau, abetted by the attitude of their parents, forms a regrettable chapter in the patriarchal history. Neither brother, and neither parent, was blameless. Jacob took unfair advantage of Esau in demanding the birthright — the right of the firstborn to pre-eminence in the tribe — but Esau also showed lack of faith in God by accepting the bargain (Gen. 25:29-34). Like many another, he was willing to sacrifice the future on the altar of the present. He argued with himself that the birthright would be meaningless if he were to die of starvation and thus, in the words of Scripture, he "despised his birthright" (Gen. 25:34). Esau's marriage to Hittite girls (Gen. 26:34) was further proof that the wishes and ideals of his parents were remote from his thoughts. The verdict of history is that Esau was a "profane person" (Heb. 12:16 A.V., R.S.V. renders "irreligious"), a man given wholly to the things of time and sense.

Rebekah and Jacob connived to deceive Isaac. The act cannot be justified morally or ethically, even though Rebekah may have sensed spiritual qualities in Jacob which were missing in Esau. The father had determined to bestow the birthright on Esau, his favored son, but Rebekah was equally determined that it should fall on Jacob. The boys were twins, but Esau had been born first and the law of primogeniture was observed in Israel under normal circumstances. When, as in the case of Jacob and, subsequently, Reuben (Gen. 49:3-4), primogeniture is not observed, the reason is given. It is clear that these are exceptional cases, and as such they demand explanation.

Isaac is presented in Hebrews 11 as a man of faith because of his confidence that God would work in the lives of his sons (and their descendants). "By faith," we read, "Isaac invoked future blessings on Jacob and Esau" (Heb. 11:20). The blessing of Esau did not compare with that of Jacob (Gen. 27:27-40), nevertheless it was prophesied that Esau-Edom would become a great people and would one day break the yoke of Jacob and lead an independent existence (Gen. 27:40).

Jacob, the deceiver, had a long, tortuous road before he became a respected patriarch and tribal father. With the twofold purpose of escaping the wrath of Esau and finding a wife for himself, he went northward to Haran where he remained for twenty years (Gen. 27:41-44; 31:38). During his flight he dreamed of a ladder reaching to heaven, and heard the voice of God renewing the covenant earlier made with Abraham and Isaac to the effect that his descendants would one day inherit all of Canaan (Gen. 28:12-14). Jacob made a vow there, at Bethel, promising to serve the Lord if He should bring him back in peace (Gen. 28:20).

The years at Haran were not marked by spiritual progress, although the blessing of God was evident in material things. Laban had outwitted Jacob by making him serve seven years for Leah, when actually Rachel was the desired wife. An additional seven years of labor were required for Rachel, but Jacob did not hesitate to spend that time in the service of her father (Gen. 29:9-30). In due time, Jacob was blessed with a large family and, in spite of Laban's craftiness, his flocks and his herds also prospered.

It was only when difficulties arose with the sons of Laban (Gen. 31:1), that Jacob determined to migrate back to Canaan with his wives, children, and possessions. Fearful of an encounter with Esau, Jacob sent his retinue across the Jabbok while he remained alone on the northern shore. There he had an experience with a nameless assailant which was to have important spiritual results. Jacob and "a man" wrestled throughout the night, but neither could down the other. The man then touched the joint of Jacob's thigh, causing him to go limp, but Jacob fought on. In some way the patriarch sensed that his mysterious assailant was God Himself, and Jacob insisted, " I will not let you go unless you bless me" (Gen. 32:26). The blessing came in the form of a new name — expressive of a new relationship — "Israel," meaning "He who strives with God," or "God strives." Jacob called the place of this encounter, "Peniel," for, he observed, "I have seen God face to face, and yet my life is preserved" (Gen. 32:24-30).

Jacob and Esau were amicably reunited, although they soon went their several ways, Esau to the region of Mount Seir, and Edom (Gen. 33:16), but Jacob to Shechem in Canaan (Gen. 33:18). After a sad experience at Shechem where Dinah, a daughter of Jacob, was defiled by one of the youths of the city and her brothers retaliated by killing its inhabitants and plundering their property, Jacob and his family moved on to Bethel. Jacob insisted that the idols which his household had accumulated be put away (Gen. 35:1-4), as they turned toward the city where God had first appeared to him twenty years before. Here, again, God confirmed the covenant (Gen. 35:9-15).

The latter years of Jacob were beset with much grief. Rivalries among his sons caused them to sell Joseph, the eldest son of his favorite wife Rachel, into slavery. Rachel herself had died in giving birth to a second son, Benjamin, and Jacob's love for Rachel was now showered on her two sons (Gen. 35:16-19; 37:3). Years later, during a time of famine, Jacob learned that Joseph was alive, and the family group was reunited. Before that, however, there were years of bitter grief.

The faith of Jacob, like that of his father, is associated, in Hebrews, with his blessing: "By faith Jacob, when dying, blessed each of the sons of Joseph, bowing in worship over the head of his staff" (Heb. 11:21). Jacob had not only uttered patriarchal blessings on his own sons (Gen. 49:1-28), but he adopted the sons of Joseph, giving Ephraim and Manasseh, each, a tribal portion (Gen. 48:17-20).

5

THE PEOPLES AMONG WHOM THE PATRIARCHS LIVED

Although we cannot assign positive dates to the Biblical patriarchs, their lives appear to span the opening half of the second millennium before Christ – roughly 2000 to 1500 B.C. Before the rise of modern archaeological studies, these years were a complete blank except for the events described in Scripture. Now, however, we are able to trace the movements of peoples in the ancient world as far back as 3000 B.C. with an amazing degree of accuracy. Abraham, instead of being at the beginning of history, now appears rather late in the history of the lands of the Fertile Crescent – the name assigned by the Egyptologist James H. Breasted to the fertile valley of the Tigris and Euphrates rivers and the coastlands of Syria and Palestine. Abraham journeyed through the Fertile Crescent and had contacts with its peoples. His descendants Isaac, Jacob, and Joseph likewise moved from Canaan northward to Paddan-aram and southward to Egypt. The culture of the patriarchs is described as seminomadic, but it was touched by some of the most advanced civilizations the world has ever seen.

1. Sumerians

By the time of the Biblical patriarchs, Sumerians had lived for more than a millennium in southern Mesopotamia in the land known to Bible students as Shinar. The Sumerians built a number of city-states including Ur, the birthplace of Abraham, Erech (Uruk) fifty miles northwest of Ur, and Lagash, fifty miles due north of Ur. The cities were ruled by men who bore the title *ensi* and served as viceroys for the gods of Sumer. The *ensi* was expected to act as "shepherd" over the flock of the patron deity of the city which he ruled. The god himself was regarded as the real king. The *ensi* had charge of practical matters such as the maintenance of the canals which made irrigation possible and the defense of the city on the field of battle.

Occasionally an *ensi* sought power beyond that of his own state and dreamed of empire. Such a ruler was Urukagina of Lagash (*ca.* twenty-fourth century B.C.) who, through conquest, became king, or *lugal* "of Lagash and Sumer." Although we do not have a law code from Urukagina, he is known as the first reformer in history. He relieved the people by reducing the fees which were charged by greedy priests and lowered prices in general throughout his realm.

The system of city-states in use by the Sumerian *ensis* was not able to meet the challenge of a dedicated empire-builder such as Sargon of Akkad. Sargon's origins are obscure. He was a Semite who rose to power in Kish, conquered all of Sumer, and then embarked on a series of conquests which took him westward to Syria. The dynasty of Sargon (*ca.* 2360-2180 B.C.) introduced the Semitic Akkadian language in place of the Sumerian tongue which had been spoken in southern Mesopotamia from the dawn of history. The tents in which the earlier Sumerians lived were replaced by huts of sun-dried brick.

Sargon's greatest successor was Naram-sin whose Victory Stele is one of the great monuments of antiquity. It commemorates a victorious campaign against a mountain people known as the Lulubi. The king's light-armed soldiers are seen advancing up the slope of a mountain with lances and standards. High in the hills, towering above them, is the king himself, wearing the horned helmet of a god and carrying a war axe and bow and arrow. His enemies are seen beneath his feet, one with an arrow piercing his throat, and another with raised hands begging for life.

Shortly after the conquests of Naram-sin, however, Akkadian power collapsed (*ca.* 2200 B.C.) under the impact of invaders from the mountain country to the northeast known as Gutium. The century of Gutian rule was one of cultural sterility, and few records of the period have survived. The defeat of the Akkadian dynasty did, however, make possible the emergence of a Sumerian renaissance which took place under the Third Dynasty of Ur.

The first king of the Third Dynasty of Ur was Ur-nammu, whose law code is the oldest currently known. Another important ruler of the period was Gudea, viceroy under one of the Ur III kings in the city of Lagash. Statuary and objects of art from the period of Gudea's rule are considered among the finest examples of Sumerian craftsmanship.

The distinction between Sumerian and Akkadian (Semite) tended to break down during the Third Dynasty of Ur (*ca.* 2060-1950 B.C.). Akkadian became the spoken language of southern Mesopotamia, with Sumerian surviving as the language of the learned, particularly in the temple. Semites became the predominant element in the population and many of the Sumerian kings of Ur actually had Semitic names and, doubtless, Semitic blood.

Abraham left Ur during the period when Sumerian culture was in the decline. Its golden period was long in the past. The people of southern Mesopotamia had known the art of writing for over a millennium and had developed social and political institutions of a high order.

2. Amorites

We read of invasions of "barbarians" into the lands of the Fertile Crescent about 2000 B.C., particularly into northern Syria and Mesopotamia. The Babylonians called these people "Amorites," a name meaning "westerners." Palestine and Syria were known as the land of the Amorites, and the Scriptures indicate that they occupied large portions of Canaan. On occasion the terms Canaanite and Amorite appear to be interchangeable.

Before entering the fertile lands of the Tigris-Euphrates valley and Palestine, Amorites lived as Bedouins in the Arabian desert. In times of weakness among the lands of the Fertile Crescent, or during periods of famine resulting from a greater scarcity of food than usual in the desert areas, nomads have emerged from the desert and conquered the more civilized peoples. Not only the Amorites, but also the Aramaeans and, in the seventh century A.D., the Islamic Arabs emerged from the desert to challenge the settled peoples in neighboring lands.

Many of the Amorite names are strikingly similar to those we meet among the Biblical Hebrews. Documents from the Amorite city of Mari, on the middle Euphrates, mention an Abam-ram (Abraham), and a Jacob-el (Jacob) as well as people known as Benjaminites. Cities include Til-Turakhi (Terah), Sarugi (Serug) and Phaliga (Peleg). They are all located in the neighborhood of Haran, the district known in the Bible as Paddan-aram ("the fields of Aram").

During the period of disorder following the end of the Third Dynasty of Ur, the Sumerian city-states were replaced by Amorite kingdoms. One of our early law codes was produced by an Amorite king of Isin named Lipit-Ishtar. He used the classical Sumerian language rather than his Amorite tongue, however.

Assyria was also ruled by an Amorite, Shamshi-adad I (*ca.* 1748-1717 B.C.), who pursued a policy of conquest, occupying the territory from the Zagros mountains to northern Syria. Shamshi-adad set up a stele to commemorate his conquest and took upon himself the grandiose title "King of the World."

Although Shamshi-adad was able to conquer the state of Mari, on the middle Euphrates, Assyrian power was ephemeral. Yasmah-adad, the son of Shamshi-adad, ruled Mari for sixteen years, but his dynasty was ousted by a native of Mari named Zimri-lim (1730-1700 B.C.) under whose leadership Mari became a major power. The borders of Mari reached from the frontiers of Babylon to the neighborhood of Carchemish. A defensive alliance was made with Babylon, and diplomatic correspondence was carried on with numerous states in Syria. The kings of the leading powers of the Mari age – Babylon, Larsa, Eshnunna, Qatna, and Aleppo – all had Amorite names with the exception of Rim-sin of Larsa.

A French expedition under André Parrot excavated the mound known as Tell el-Hariri which marks the spot of ancient Mari, on the middle Euphrates. The 20,000 clay tablets found there deal with military, diplomatic, and administrative matters, and provide primary source material for the study of life during the Patriarchal Age.

Mari boasted a magnificent temple to Ishtar which has been studied by the archaeologists. Ishtar was believed to have given a staff and ring, emblems of authority, to the king of Mari. The palace of Zimri-Lim is one of the best preserved structures in the Near East. It covered more than fifteen acres and was equipped with vast courts, suites of rooms, a bathroom, kitchen, and chapel. The throne room was adorned with frescoes such as appear in the great palaces of the later Assyrian rulers. The Mari palace not only made provision for the royal family and the state officials, but it also contained a school for the scribes who served as royal secretaries.

The Mari age was one of great mobility. Traders journeyed to Anatolia in Asia Minor, to Byblos and Ugarit on the Mediterranean coast, and overseas to Cyprus and Crete.

The power of Mari waned, however, before another Amorite ruler, Hammurabi of Babylon (1728-1686 B.C.). Hammurabi was forceful on the field of battle as well as efficient in affairs of government. He annexed the states of Isin and Larsa, brought Assyria into subjection, and then turned his attention to Mari. Zimri-lim, the last king of Mari, was defeated by Hammurabi (1697 B.C.) and a few years later his capital was completely destroyed. Mari never arose from the ashes.

Many empires of antiquity covered more territory than that of Hammurabi, but few have been culturally more significant. Hammurabi's Babylon has left us a legacy of literature in a variety of areas: common letters and contracts, major epics dealing with the creation of the world and the flood, mathematical treatises, astronomical texts, grammars, dictionaries, and – most famous of all – the law code of the king, himself.

Although the dynasty of Hammurabi persisted for a century and a half after the death of the great lawgiver, its day of real power was short lived. Conquered states began to assert their independence during the reign of Hammurabi's successor, Samsu-iluna (1685-1648 B.C.) Trouble also came from without when a little-known people who are termed Kassites (or Cossaeans) appeared in southern Mesopotamia and challenged the power of Babylon.

3. Hurrians

During the Patriarchal Age large numbers of people known as Hurrians (Biblical Horites) entered the Fertile Crescent, presumably from the mountains of Armenia. By the sixteenth century B.C., Hurrians had large settlements in Upper Mesopotamia, Syria, and Palestine. The town of Nuzi, southeast of Nineveh, was almost solidly Hurrian. From the cuneiform tablets discovered at Nuzi we learn something of the language and customs of the Hurrians, although they seem to have adopted much of the older Amorite culture of the area. These tablets, written in the Semitic Akkadian language, illustrate many of the social customs and attitudes which find expression in Hammurabi's law code and in the daily life of the Biblical patriarchs.

Late in the sixteenth century a kingdom known as Mitanni dominated northern Mesopotamia between the Mediterranean and Media. The state had a predominantly Hurrian population, although its rulers bore Indo-Aryan names. The Indo-Aryans, who appear to have been associated with the Hurrians in their tribal movements, introduced the chariot into the techniques of warfare. A class of chariot-warriors known as *maryannu* occupied the upper strata of society.

The Hurrians and the Indo-Aryans appear to have intermarried with the result that the two peoples became, for all practical purposes, one. About 1500 B.C. their state of Mitanni held the balance of power between the Hittite Empire and Egypt.

4. Hapiru

A people known as Hapiru (sometimes written ʿApiru or Ḫabiru) appear in many parts of the Near East during patriarchal times. They are mentioned in tablets from the Third Dynasty of Ur, from Babylon, and from the Hittite territory of Asia Minor. We read of them in nineteenth century Anatolia, eighteenth century Mari, fifteenth century Nuzi, and fourteenth century Ras Shamra (Ugarit). They are frequently mentioned in the Tell el-Amarna tablets from fourteenth century Egypt and in numerous other Egyptian writings of the Empire Period – the fifteenth to the twelfth centuries B.C.

The Hapiru not only turn up in a variety of places; they serve in many different capacities. In times of peace they are found working in the widely scattered communities of the Near East. Sometimes they appear as clients to men of the upper classes and, in times of adversity we read of Hapiru selling themselves into slavery. The Nuzi tablets show that the status of slave might be preferred to that of a free man because of the economic security it brought. Hapiru in Egypt served as slaves on the royal building projects, as did the Biblical Hebrews (cf. Exod. 1:11).

In unsettled periods the Hapiru usually appear as a seminomadic people who stage periodic raids on the settled communities. The Amarna Letters contain appeals from kings of Canaanite city states (including Jerusalem) for help from Egypt to repel the invading Hapiru. Sometimes the Hapiru served as mercenary soldiers, hiring themselves out to the highest bidder.

Who were these Hapiru? Most of their names are Semitic, but there are numerous exceptions. They do not conform to the pattern of an ethnic group. George Mendenhall, of the University of Michigan, suggests that the term Hapiru designates a people living beyond the bounds of a given community (i.e. a people without citizenship). They were not subject to the laws and mores of the settled peoples, hence were regarded as outsiders. The Near East had developed a highly organized social structure, but the Hapiru were not a part of it. Sometimes they made their peace with the ruling society, and sometimes they were outlaws.

The similarity of the name Hebrew to Hapiru may not be accidental. Although in modern usage the words Hebrew and Israelite are synonymous, this is not uniformly true in Scripture. The term Hebrew is rarely used, and then usually in contexts in which Israelites identify themselves to foreigners, or by foreigners in referring to Israelites. In the book of Genesis the term is used once of Abraham and several times in the account of Joseph in Egypt. When a confederacy of kings from the East defeated the king of Sodom and his allies, one of those who had escaped brought word of the capture of Lot to "Abram the Hebrew" (Gen. 14:13). Potiphar's wife, in falsely accusing Joseph, exclaimed, "See, he has brought among us a Hebrew to insult us" (Gen. 39:14, 17). In stating his case before Pharaoh, Joseph identified himself with the statement, "For I was indeed stolen out of the land of the Hebrews . . . " (Gen. 40:15). When Pharaoh's daughter looked upon the infant Moses, she exclaimed, "This is one of the Hebrews' children" (Exod. 2:6).

The word Hebrew continued in use down to the time of the wars with the Philistines. When the Israelites brought the sacred ark to the battlefield at Aphek, the Philistines heard the shout of the warriors and asked, "What does this great shouting in the camp of the Hebrews mean?" (I Sam. 4:6). Encouraging their own forces to renewed efforts to resist the Israelites, the Philistine leaders exclaimed, "Take courage and acquit yourselves like men, O Philistines, lest you become slaves to the Hebrews, as they have been to you" (I Sam. 4:9).

When the prophet Jonah was confronted by his angry shipmates with the demand that he identify himself, he replied, "I am a Hebrew, and I fear the Lord of heaven, who made the sea and the dry land" (Jonah 1:9). Such usage becomes rare, however, in the latter part of the Old Testament.

We cannot identify the Biblical Hebrews with the Hapiru of the ancient cuneiform literature but there are evident relationships between the two peoples. The Israelites in their early history were looked upon as an alien people, and from the standpoint of Canaanites and Egyptians they were doubtless looked upon as Hapiru. The Israelite conquest of Canaan was certainly regarded as an Hapiru invasion, although chronological considerations argue against identification of the events of the book of Joshua with the invasions described in the Amarna Letters. Among the Hapiru who were slaves in Egypt during the reign of Pharaoh Ramesses II there may have been many whom we know as Hebrews or Israelites.

5. Egypt

Our knowledge of ancient Egypt parallels that of Sumer. Although located at opposite ends of the Fertile Crescent and differing in cultural inheritance, Egyptians and Sumerians both made their appearance in history about 3000 B.C.

As in the case of the Sumerians, we are unable to say much concerning the racial affinities of the Egyptians. Mizraim, the son of Ham in the Biblical Table of Nations (Gen. 10), gives us our Hebrew name for Egypt. This causes us to speak of Egyptians as Hamites, whereas we speak of the Israelites and many of their neighbors as Semites. In modern usage the terms Hamitic and Semitic are used to describe languages rather than racial characteristics. People who spoke Semitic languages are termed Semites, although we know that many non-Semitic peoples were incorporated into the Semitic cultures of the ancient world. Similarly the peoples which we term Hamites have a variety of racial strains. Earlier historians thought of the Egyptians as negroid, but this view has been abandoned. J. H. Breasted in his monumental *History of Egypt* observes, "At most, he (i.e. the Egyptian) may be slightly tinctured with negro blood."[1]

At the time when hieroglyphic writing first appeared (*ca.* 3000 B.C.), Egypt was already a highly cultured country. We do not learn of its past from the excavation of mounds, as in ancient Sumer, but from the study of tombs and burial chambers built in the desert which stretches interminably on both sides of the Nile valley. The dryness of the desert made it unsuitable for cultivation, but it was an ideal climate for the preservation of the bodies and artifacts of the ancient Egyptians. Mummified bodies of Pharaohs and their servants, along with quantities of jewelry, stone vases, copper vessels and other objects have been found there. Even wood, which would normally have rotted away centuries ago, has been preserved in the dry desert.

The period between the twenty-ninth and the twenty-third centuries B.C. is known as the Old Kingdom, a period when the Pharaoh reigned with absolute power as god and king.

1. James Henry Breasted, *A History of Egypt,* p. 26.

Records indicate that many of these rulers were educated men. They could read and write, direct mining operations in the Sinai peninsula and dispatch orders to their military commanders at Nubia, south of Egypt, and Punt on the Red Sea. Ministers and engineers sought audience with the Pharaohs to discuss the needs of the land. Since Egypt has no rainfall, but is dependent for irrigation on the annual floods resulting from the overflow of the Nile River, considerable attention had to be given to irrigation problems. This dependence of all the Egyptians on the Nile doubtless helps to account for the strength of the government. Only through collective effort could the people hope to survive.

The Pharaohs, however, had personal concerns and frequently employed architects to plan extensive royal estates. During the twenty-sixth and the twenty-fifth centuries a series of immense pyramids was built at great expense of material and labor. These pyramids are esteemed among the wonders of the ancient world. They had been standing for five hundred years when Abraham sojourned in Egypt, and they are standing today.

The first pyramid was designed by Imhotep, a renowned priest who served as architect for Pharaoh Djoser. The step pyramid which he constructed at Saqqara is the earliest large stone structure in history. It comprises a large stone burial vault (known as a mastaba) on which five successive layers were built in the form of steps. The terraced monument which resulted was one hundred ninety feet high.

The largest of the pyramids was built by a Pharaoh named Khufu, or Cheops, founder of the Egyptian Fourth Dynasty. The square base of his pyramid covered thirteen acres. It was 481 feet high and contained 2,300,000 blocks of yellow limestone, each averaging two and one-half tons. Herodotus, the Greek historian, claimed that the laborers worked in groups of 100,000 men. The precision with which the building was erected amazes even the mind steeped in precision instruments and exact formulae.

A second pyramid at Giza was built by Khafre (Chephren), the successor of Khufu, near which was a sphinx with the representation of Khafre's head on the body of a reclining lion. Later Pharaohs continued to build pyramids, but the size and grandeur gradually diminished. The pyramids were built as tombs for the Pharaohs, and the energy expended on them proved to be an unproductive drain upon the national economy. The pyramids were luxuries which the nation could ill afford.

The twenty-second and twenty-first centuries B.C. mark a period of Egyptian history known as the "First Intermediate Period." Our sources of information for this time are scanty, but it appears that the nobles grew in power at the expense of the central government. Resentment against oppression found expression in the desecration of the tombs of Old Kingdom Pharaohs. Temples were pillaged and their works of art were subjected to systematic and determined vandalism. One of the nobles boasted, "I rescued my city in the day of violence from the terrors of the royal house."[2]

Although Egyptian Pharaohs were never again to have the absolute power which they enjoyed during the Pyramid Age, a strong central government was established in the twenty-first century. This government, known as the Middle Kingdom, lasted until the eighteenth century when Egypt was overrun by the Hyksos invaders from Asia.

The patriarch Abraham is not mentioned by name but there is abundant evidence of contacts between Egyptians and Semites during the age of the Middle Kingdom. A tomb painting at Beni Hasan, 169 miles south of Cairo, depicts a powerful noble of the Middle Kingdom, Khnumhotep, welcoming a group of desert Semites who are bringing gifts and seeking trade. The inscription which accompanies the painting reads, "The arrival, bringing eye-paint, which thirty-seven Asiatics bring to him." The leader of the Semites is identified as, "Sheik of the highlands, Ibshe."

During the Middle Kingdom, the god of Thebes, the capital city, lost his provincial character and became the god of the whole land. He was identified with the sun god, Re, and bore the combined title, "Amon-Re, King of the Gods." A massive temple to Amon-Re was built at Karnak, near Thebes. Construction was continued for a period of over two millennia – from the Middle Kingdom of Egypt until Roman times. Ultimately the priests of Amon-Re achieved a power which compared with that of the Pharaoh, himself.

In the interest of greater efficiency, the capital of Egypt was moved from Thebes to Memphis at the head of the Delta. In this way more effective control could be maintained over the "two Egypts" – Lower Egypt, or the Delta, and Upper Egypt, the Nile Valley to the borders of Nubia at the First Cataract. Efficient palace schools were maintained there in order to train officials for their political posts.

---

2. James Henry Breasted, *Ancient Records of Egypt,* I, p. 690.

Bronze became a basic metal in the Egyptian economy, and the Pharaohs of the Middle Kingdom again exploited the copper mines in the Sinai region. Beautiful pieces of feminine jewelry date from this period. Although not as original in design as the work of the Old Kingdom masters, Middle Kingdom artists maintained an excellent standard of work.

Of more utilitarian value was the program of Middle Kingdom Pharaohs to expand the amount of cultivable land in the area southwest of Memphis known as the Faiyum. A huge embankment was built there to serve as a catch basin for the waters of the Nile at the time of the annual inundation. In this way an estimated twenty-seven thousand acres of cultivable land were added to the Faiyum district.

Middle Kingdom Egypt produced some of the great masterpieces of world literature. One of these is the tale of Sinuhe, an Egyptian who fled to Canaan and prospered there. The land of Canaan was barbaric, however, in comparison with Egypt, and Sinuhe was happy to return to his home country that he might die there and be buried in a pyramid!

Another Middle Egyptian story recounts the adventures of the sole survivor of a storm at sea. The Shipwrecked Sailor, who gives his name to the story, was cast ashore on a magical island ruled by a giant serpent who had superhuman power and wisdom. The story relates how the serpent was kind to the sailor and sent him home in a ship which materialized according to the serpent's prophecy. The serpent also told the sailor that he would never see the island again, ". . . it will have become water." The island, the story tells us, disappeared, and no one could ever disprove the sailor's yarn. This is regarded as one of the earliest examples of the short story.

A third Middle Kingdom work, of an entirely different variety, is the Tale of the Eloquent Peasant. A wronged farmer presented his case before the magistrate with such eloquence that a decision was deferred. The peasant's eloquent appeals for justice were recorded for the amusement of the king — and of the modern reader!

Although the ancient Egyptians were a religious people, skepticism was not lacking. The Song of the Harper tells of the minstrel who sang about the vanity of life to the guests at a banquet. Since we cannot take our possessions with us when we leave the world, the harper suggests that we eat, drink, and be merry.

Before the end of the eighteenth century, Egyptian power was again in decline. The contention for power on the part of rival dynasties opened the way for invasion by foreigners from Asia known as the Hyksos.

The name Hyksos, long thought to have meant "shepherd kings," is now taken to be a contraction of words meaning "rulers of foreign lands." They worshiped the Canaanite gods, notably Baal, and are thought to have been Canaanite and Amorite princes from Syria and Palestine. The Hyksos rulers established their capital at Avaris (Tanis), in the Delta near the northeastern frontier. In this way they were close to their Asiatic domains as well as the land of Egypt.

The Hyksos were hated by the native Egyptians, with the result that monuments of their rule were destroyed. Josephus, the Jewish historian of the first century A.D., records a passage from Manetho, an Egyptian historian of about 300 B.C., who wrote of the Hyksos conquerors:

> In his reign (i.e. Pharaoh Titimaeus), for what cause I know not, a blast of God smote us; and, unexpectedly, from the regions of the east, invaders of obscure race marched in confidence of victory against our land. By main force they easily seized it without striking a blow; and having overpowered the rulers of the land, they then burned our cities ruthlessly, razed to the ground the temples of the gods, and treated all the natives with a cruel hostility.... Finally they appointed as king one of their number whose name was Salitis.

Hated as the Hyksos rulers were, they brought important changes into Egyptian life. Egypt had thought of itself as the center of culture and refinement, and looked with disdain on foreign "barbarians." The Hyksos, by humiliating Egypt, made the Egyptians conscious of the fact that there were other people in the world and that they must, in one way or another, be reckoned with. The Hyksos introduced the war chariot into Egypt. Within a few years Egyptian chariots would be turned against the Asiatics.

The Hyksos were expelled from Egypt about 1570 B.C. The liberator was Amosis (1570-1546) whose brother Kamose had succeeded in raising an army and pushing the Hyksos into the eastern Delta where they consolidated their forces at Avaris, their capital. Kamose did not live to see the final defeat of the Hyksos, but his brother carried on the fight, seized Avaris, and drove the Hyksos from Egypt. Amosis pursued them to southern Palestine where he laid siege to their fortress at Sharuhen. After a three year siege, Sharuhen fell and the Hyksos threat to Egypt was over.

With Amosis the New Kingdom, or Empire period of Egyptian history began, the period graphically described in the title of a book by George Steindorff and Keith Seele, *When Egypt Ruled the East.* After his victory at Sharuhen, Amosis turned his attention to Nubia, the land south of Egypt. The Hyksos had never been able to subdue Nubia, but Amosis did so, and the Egyptian Empire was begun. Before the end of the Empire Period, (*ca.* 1100 B.C.), Egyptian power reached the Euphrates, and Egyptian armies were a familiar sight in Syria and Palestine.

The descent of Joseph and, later, of his father and brothers, had important repercussions in later Israelite history. The Pharaoh under whom Joseph served as Prime Minister is not named, however, and we have no means of positive identification. Many scholars consider the period of Hyksos rule to be the logical time to place the account of another Semite, Joseph, rising to power in Egypt. The fact that so little is known about the Hyksos period makes it impossible for us to be certain.

It is, of course, also possible that Joseph entered Egypt during the latter years of the Middle Kingdom. The Beni Hasan inscription indicates that Semites were not strangers in Egypt, and it is conceivable that Joseph came there at that time. The fact that shepherds were described as an abomination to the Egyptians (Gen. 46:34) and that the Egyptians would not eat with the Hebrews (Gen. 43:32) may suggest that we are dealing with a native dynasty. On the other hand, the Hyksos rulers probably adopted many of the customs and attitudes of the people they conquered. The fact that the Pharaoh lived fairly close to Goshen, where Joseph's family was permitted to settle (Gen. 46:31; 47:10), appears to argue for a time when the capital was in the Delta, as it was during the Hyksos period.

6

THE CITIES OF THE PATRIARCHS

The Biblical patriarchs spent most of their lives "in tents" living a seminomadic life. Their wealth was in herds and flocks rather than real estate.

If Abraham and his descendants lived in the Palestinian Negev rather than the cultural centers of the Fertile Crescent, it was from choice rather than necessity. The Biblical record tells us that the father of the Israelite nation left Ur of the Chaldees with his father, Terah. Subsequently they sojourned in Haran before Abraham began the seminomadic life in Canaan.

1. Ur of the Chaldees

The Sumerian city of Ur, in southern Mesopotamia, was first excavated by the British consul at Basra, J. E. Taylor, in 1854. At that time all that was left of the once great city was a mound known in Arabic as *al Muqayyar* ("the mound of pitch"). Excavations were resumed by H. R. Hall in 1918, and again by Sir Leonard Wooley in 1922.

The title "Ur of the Chaldees" identifies the city as having been located in the land which was later called Chaldaea. One of the Chaldaean, or Neo-Babylonian kings, Nabonidus, (555-539 B.C.) actually gave attention to rebuilding the city of Ur which had been in ruins for centuries.

The Ur of the book of Genesis was a thriving cultural center of Sumerian life. Its history is known to go back to the Early Bronze Age (3000-2100 B.C.). Several hundred clay tablets discovered at Ur represent the culture of the Classical Sumerian period (2800-2700 B.C.).

An ancient Sumerian document, known as the King List, lists rulers who lived both before and after the flood, described in another cuneiform tablet. The third dynasty of kings after the flood, according to the King List, came from Ur. Mes-anni-padda was the name of the first of these kings.

Our appreciation of the art of ancient Ur has been greatly increased since the discovery, by Woolley, of the so-called royal cemeteries which are thought to date about 2500 B.C. A noble lady, popularly named Queen Shubad, was buried there along with her impressive head attire, jewelry, a gold tumbler and cup. There was a tragic side to the royal tombs, however. The evidences of Sumerian culture and refinement were countered by evidence that attendants were sacrificed at the time of the funeral of their masters. It was evidently felt that faithful servants should accompany their earthly masters into the next world.

The Sumerians of Ur shared the fate of others of their race when Sargon of Akkad founded a Semitic dynasty in southern Mesopotamia (2360-2180 B.C.). Although Ur was no longer a major political center, Woolley did find remains of the city dating from the time of Sargon's rule.

A brief Sumerian renaissance (2070-1960 B.C.) brought Ur to the fore again. Ur-nammu is accounted first king of the Third Dynasty of Ur which lasted until an Amorite from Mari on the middle Euphrates, Ishbi-irra by name, overran the Sumerian territory and occupied Isin (1960-1830 B.C.). At the same time a group of Elamites crossed the Tigris and established their vassal, Naplanum, on the throne of Larsa.

During the Third Dynasty of Ur a number of important buildings were erected. The moon god Nanna (Semitic, Sin), the patron deity of Ur was honored with a beautiful temple built on a specially constructed temple tower known as a ziggurat. Another temple was built for Nanna's consort, Nin-gal. A treasury building and a palace for the high priestess also adorned the city during the Ur III period.

The Elamites who had seized Larsa extended their power over Ur in the years which followed the Third Dynasty of Ur. Subsequently Rim-sin of Larsa was conquered by the sixth king of the first dynasty of Babylon, (1728-1686 B.C.), the great lawgiver Hammurabi. Ur rebelled, however, during the reign of Samsu-illuna, Hammurabi's son. The city was destroyed and, in spite of the efforts of Nabonidus to rebuild it over a millennium later, it never again became a place of importance.

It would be interesting to know just when "the God of glory appeared unto our father Abraham when he was in Mesopotamia, before he dwelt in Haran," but we do not have exact chronologies before the days of the Israelite kingdom (*ca.* 1000 B.C.). Some Biblical scholars suggest that Ur-nammu was the ruler of Ur during the time of Abraham. Did Abraham look upon the great Ziggurat which Ur-Nammu built? Did he know anything of the law code of this ruler who called himself "king of Sumer and Akkad?" We cannot know for sure.

Even if the Ur of Abraham's lifetime was earlier or later than Ur-Nammu, it was a cultural and religious center of considerable importance. Jewish tradition suggests that Abraham's ancestors had been idol-makers at Ur. Scripture, while silent on such details, does make it clear that the ancestors of the Biblical patriarchs served "other gods" before they came to know the true God. Abraham turned his back on a highly civilized environment when he left Ur in obedience to the command of the Lord.

2. Haran

Travelers between southern Mesopotamia and Palestine did not journey through the desert but took the longer route around the Fertile Crescent. Abraham, with Terah, his father set out along the familiar road northward from Ur.

The migration from Ur took Abraham and his father to Haran, a northern Mesopotamian city on the Bilikh River about sixty miles from its entrance into the Euphrates. The word Haran means "road" and the city was located on an important caravan route connecting Nineveh and Babylon with Damascus, Tyre, and Egypt. Haran, like Ur, was devoted to the worship of the Moon God. People from Ur would feel at home there, and the temptation was great to forego the uncertain journey into Canaan. Terah, Abraham's father, got no farther than Haran, but Abraham himself moved on to Canaan.

Shortly before and after 2000 B.C., a nomadic people known as Amorites ("westerners") invaded the settled areas of the Near East. The Aramaeans, to whom Laban was related (Gen. 31:20), are thought to have been an Amorite people. The Israelites, too, acknowledged their Aramaean origin in the confession, "A wandering Aramaean was my father" (Deut. 26:5). It is of interest that Haran is known to have been an Amorite state shortly after 2000 B.C.

The region around Haran was subsequently thought of as the ancestral home of Abraham's family. It is known as Paddan-aram ("Field of Aram") or Aram-naharaim ("Aram of the Two Rivers" or "Mesopotamia"). To this area Abraham sent a trusted servant to secure a suitable bride for Isaac, and here Jacob fled to escape the wrath of Esau and to marry a daughter of Laban. Actually he was married to both Leah and Rachel, and remained about twenty years before returning to Canaan.

3. The Cities of Canaan

Abraham moved on from Haran into the land of Canaan. He first pitched his tent under the oak (or terebinth) of Moreh at Shechem. The site of Shechem (modern *Tell Balatah*) is known to have been an important Canaanite city between 2000 and 1800 B.C., and again between 1400 and 1200 B.C. Water was a perennial problem in Canaan, and the fact that "Jacob's well" was in the Shechem area made it a particularly attractive site.

Tell Balatah is being systematically excavated by the Drew-McCormick Expedition which is heir to the work of German scholars who conducted seven campaigns there between 1913 and 1934. Palaces and streets have been discovered which date to the eighteenth, and the first half of the seventeenth centuries B.C. In his report in the *Biblical Archaeologist,* Edward F. Campbell, Jr., observes: "The one hundred years which immediately preceded the coming of the Hyksos to Shechem appear to have seen lively building activity indeed. Who knows but that the patriarch Joseph saw these now ruined palaces when they were dominating the western edge of the city?"[1]

Beer-sheba is also noted for its wells, although the city has not been excavated. The city is still the market center for the Negev, a position which it doubtless had since patriarchal times. Abraham, Isaac, and Jacob all spent some portion of their lives in Beer-sheba.

The Tell el-Amarna tablets from fifteenth century Egypt speak of the city of *Rubuti* ("the four") which seems to be the equivalent of the Biblical Kirjath-arba ("city of four," or "tetrapolis"). This city in southern Palestine, nineteen miles southwest of Jerusalem, is best known to us as Hebron ("the league") a city which, according to Numbers 13:22 was built "seven years before Zoan in Egypt."

Zoan, known at different times as Avaris and Tanis, was rebuilt by the Hyksos rulers of Egypt about 1700 B.C. George Ernest Wright of Harvard suggests that this was the date which

---

1. Edward F. Campbell, Jr., "Excavation at Shechem, 1960," *The Biblical Archaeologist* XXIII, 4, p. 110.

the sacred historian had in mind when describing the age of Hebron. If this is so, the city of Hebron was built after the time of Abraham, which would agree with the fact that the Patriarch was associated with Mamre, a plain near Hebron, rather than the city itself.

Twelve miles north of Jerusalem was the city of Luz, subsequently named Bethel (Gen. 28:19). Here Abraham built his first altar when he arrived in Canaan (Gen. 12:8) and, later, the fugitive Jacob dreamed of an open heaven and a ladder with angels bringing a message of divine encouragement (Gen. 28:11-13, 22).

The site of Bethel was excavated in 1934 by an expedition directed by Professor W. F. Albright. Pottery evidence indicates that the city was occupied during the twenty-first century B.C. The most interesting discoveries, however, come from the period subsequent to that of the patriarchs. Remains of a city wall from the sixteenth century B.C. have been found. The quality of the masonry of these walls and the houses of the period, is higher than that of any other Palestinian structures.

Both Abraham and Isaac had important dealings with the king of the Philistine city-state known as Gerar, identified with *Tell el-Jemmeh* in southern Palestine. Like Haran, Gerar was situated along a rich caravan route and, for that reason, had a thriving economy. Excavations by Sir Flinders Petrie have shown the diversity of objects used by the citizens of Gerar from the sixth to the fourth centuries B.C. Its importance during patriarchal times is indicated in the Biblical record (Gen. 20:1-18; Gen. 26:1-22).

7

CANAAN DURING PATRIARCHAL TIMES

The land to which Abraham migrated is known in the Pentateuch as the land of Canaan. The peoples of the land, although of varying ethnic backgrounds, are frequently given the collective name of Canaanites. Our knowledge of these people and the culture they represent has been greatly increased as a result of modern archaeological work. Our prime source of first hand information has been the literature from Ras Shamra, ancient Ugarit, discovered and deciphered in the years since 1929.

The etymology and significance of the name Canaan has been the subject of considerable speculation. George Adam Smith in his classical *Historical Geography of the Holy Land* relates the word Canaan to the Hebrew root *kanan* which means "to be humbled" or "to be made low." In this sense, Canaanites would be "lowlanders."

Others derive the word Canaan from the word for "purple dye" for which Canaan, especially the northern part, was once famous. Justification for this viewpoint comes from the Greeks who called the people *Phoinikes,* plural of *Phoinix;* and their land *Phoinike,* words which appear to be related to the word *phoinios,* "blood-red." This appears to refer to the reddish-purple dye which the Phoenicians extracted from the murex shellfish and made their principal article of export.

As a matter of fact the Phoenicians considered themselves Canaanites throughout their history in Syria, and their Carthaginian descendants did so in Africa as late as the fifth century A.D. Augustine states that in his time the Carthaginian peasants, when questioned concerning their race, answered, *"Chanani."*

The identification of the Canaanites with "lowlanders" as opposed to the Amorites, and, later, the Israelites who settled in the "highlands," is attractive, but the Greek usage seems to argue for a name which developed from the commercial side of Canaanite life. It is possible, of course, that folk etymology has been at work, and that the meaning of the name Canaan has been variously interpreted at different periods of history. W. F. Albright suggests that Phoenician sailors were given their name because of their sunburned skin.

1. Pre-historic Canaanites

Some of the earliest of human remains come from caves near Mount Carmel. Relics discovered there include roughly chopped and irregularly flaked flints which were used as fist hatchets. Fragments were chipped from a core of flint to make the hatchet easy to grasp for cutting or pounding. Artistic ability is seen in a head of a bull carved in bone which was discovered in one of the caves.

During the two millennia before the dawn of history (*ca.* 5000-3000 B.C.) there is evidence that the inhabitants of Canaan had begun to settle in towns and villages. Permanent houses with red painted floors were found by the Jericho expedition of 1935-36. At Teleilat el-Ghassul, four and one-half miles north of the Dead Sea, houses of the same period had foundations of uncut stone and walls of mud brick. Pottery was usually hand made, but there is evidence that the potter's wheel was known. Pavements were made of stone. Numerous flint implements, including polished axes, were discovered, but we know that copper was also in use before the beginnings of Canaanite history.

The relationship of these prehistoric peoples to the historic Canaanites is, of course, problematical. The land of Canaan witnessed a variety of ethnic movements, and the Scriptures speak not only of Canaanites but also of Jebusites, Hittites, Girgashites, Horites, Hivites, Amorites, and many others.

2. Early Cities of Canaan

Early in the Patriarchal Age (the nineteenth century B.C.) we read of many cities of considerable size in Canaan. Gezer was surrounded by strong walls and seems to have been an Egyptian outpost during patriarchal times. Egyptian statues and other objects were discovered there.

Another great city was Megiddo, which guards the strategic pass from the Plain of Sharon through the Valley of Esdraelon to the Jordan valley. A "high place" of Megiddo was used for the offering of sacrifices to the gods of Canaan about the time Abraham was bearing testimony to the faithfulness of the Lord as a sojourner in Shechem, Bethel, and Beer-sheba.

The mound of Megiddo (modern *Tell el Mutesellim*) has been excavated, first by the Deutsche Orientgesellschaft and, since 1925, by the Oriental Institute of the University of Chicago. A city is known to have been situated there as early as 3500 B.C. A brick wall and gate are dated to about 1800 B.C., when the city was occupied by Canaanites. It was not until the time of Solomon that Megiddo became an Israelite stronghold (I Kings 9:15).

During the patriarchal period the towns of Transjordan and the valley of the Jordan were also flourishing. Nelson Glueck, the noted Palestinian archaeologist and president of Hebrew Union College, made a survey of the area east and south of the Dead Sea during the years 1932 to 1939. His studies indicated that the nomadic peoples of that area had lived in villages prior to 2000 B.C., but that the villages were abandoned during the twentieth or nineteenth centuries. This appears to be a historical reflection of the events described in the book of Genesis when Sodom, Gomorrah, and the cities of the plain were destroyed. The area seems to have suffered from a tremendous earthquake about that time.

W. F. Albright has shown that Sodom, Gomorrah, and Zoar are probably beneath the shallow waters at the southern tip of the Dead Sea. Two sites nearby were excavated, and Albright concluded that they were abandoned about the twentieth century B.C. Before the destruction of Sodom and Gomorrah the area was a flourishing center of civilization. Lot felt it to be the most desirable portion of Canaan (Gen. 13:5-13).

3. An Egyptian in Canaan

From the Patriarchal Age we have a first-hand account of Canaan as it appeared to an Egyptian refugee named Sinuhe. How much of the Sinuhe story is fact and how much fiction we may never know. If it was written by a stay-at-home Egyptian, he had an excellent knowledge of both the geography and the social structure of Canaan.

The events of the story begin about 1950 B.C. when King Amenemhet died and his eldest son, Sesostris, took the throne. Sinuhe never quite explains why he had to leave Egypt, but leave it he did. After some harrowing experiences in Egypt itself, Sinuhe reached the "Walls of the Ruler," built to protect the northeast frontier of Egypt from invasion by the Asiatics. This seems to be the wall ("Shur") to which Hagar was fleeing after she left the home of Abraham. The Israelites at the time of the Exodus were directed southward into the Sinai peninsula so that they would not be attacked on the heavily traveled coastal route.

An individual, such as Sinuhe, would be better able to elude the Egyptian garrison than would the Israelite encampment. Sinuhe states that he crouched under a bush during the day and eluded the watch at the wall under cover of night.

Once he had escaped the Egyptian garrisons, Sinuhe had no serious problems. He was hospitably received by a Bedouin sheikh who had been in Egypt. Refreshments of water and boiled milk were offered the weary traveler.

Sinuhe spent some time at Byblos, on the Phoenician coast and in a land known as Kedem. The word itself means "east" and it is thought to refer here to the desert region east of Damascus. After spending a half year there he was invited to come to Upper Retjenu, evidently a name for the mountainous part of Palestine. There he soon achieved high rank. The local king gave his eldest daughter to Sinuhe in marriage and allowed him to choose some of the country for himself.

Waxing eloquent concerning this "land of Ya'a," Sinuhe exclaimed:

> It is a good land, Ya'a by name, figs and grapes are in it; it has more wine than water, it has much honey and olive oil in plenty; all fruits are upon its trees; limitless barley and spelt are there, and all kinds of herds and flocks.

A tribe was assigned to Sinuhe, who became a petty ruler in Canaan. He describes his food: wine, boiled meat, roast fowl, and the game of the desert. Milk, he says, was used in cooking. This diet, we should observe, was hardly typical of patriarchal Canaan. Sinuhe was a chieftain and a royal favorite, so he was provided with special fare.

Before long Sinuhe gained a reputation for his prowess on the field of battle. He was challenged, however, by the local Goliath but Sinuhe's reputation was vindicated. An arrow hit the assailant in the neck and Sinuhe killed the challenger with his own battle axe.

Sinuhe's successes in Canaan did not dim his love for Egypt, however. When he received a letter inviting him to return home, he eagerly prepared to leave for Egypt. He turned over his property to his children and, accompanied by attendants, started on the long journey. At the Roads of Horus, near modern Kantara, he met the frontier patrol which sent word to the Pharaoh that Sinuhe had arrived. The Bedouins who had accompanied Sinuhe to Egypt were given gifts and sent home. Sinuhe, himself, was impressed by all that he saw. Egypt was a land of efficiency: "Every serving-man was at his task."

Egyptian clothes were exchanged for the rough Bedouin garments which Sinuhe was wearing. He says: "A burden was given back to the desert – my clothes to the Sandfarers. I was clothed in fine linen, and anointed with fine oil; I lay down at night upon a bed. I gave the sand to those who dwell on it, and wood oil to him who would anoint himself with it."

In connection with this transformation, designed to make Sinuhe a good Egyptian again, we read, "I was shaved and my hair was combed." Some centuries later before an audience with the reigning Pharaoh we read of Joseph: ". . . they brought him hastily out of the dungeon, and he shaved himself, and changed his raiment" (Gen. 41:14). Semites were normally bearded, but Egyptians were clean shaven. Joseph also was given "vestures of fine linen" (Gen. 41:42) in keeping with the post which was assigned to him in Egypt.

The crowning achievement of Sinuhe's return to Egypt was the stone pyramid which was built for him. Burial in Canaan was quite simple. The body was placed in a cloth and buried in the ground. Egypt, however, made a great to-do over funerals. Draughtsmen designed the pyramid, sculptors carved it, and builders took the responsibility of seeing that everything was done properly. Sinuhe can be considered a success, according to Egyptian standards. He was buried in a pyramid.

The desire to be buried in one's homeland was not exclusively Egyptian, of course. Jacob had charged his sons: "Bury me with my fathers in the cave that is in the field of Ephron the Hittite" (Gen. 49:29). Joseph, too, said to his fellow-Israelites, "God shall surely visit you, and ye shall carry up my bones from hence." (Gen. 50:25). Jacob's remains were taken to Canaan shortly after he died, but Joseph was embalmed (or mummified) and "put in a coffin in Egypt" (Gen. 50:26) until the time of the Exodus.

4. Agriculture

Agriculture is dependent upon fertile soil. In Canaan this poses a problem because of the long periods when there is no rain. Throughout the summer the fields are parched, but the "former rains" begin late in September or early in October. This makes possible a time of planting and ploughing in the fall of the year. The winter is wet with occasional snow as far south as Bethlehem. In March and April a series of heavy showers known as the "latter rains" soak the fields and fill empty cisterns. Following the latter rains the dry summer begins.

Compared with the fertile Nile valley and the lands drained by the Tigris and Euphrates, Canaan was a land which held little promise. The Biblical records speak of numerous famines, often accompanied by migrations of people in search of food. During the time of Joseph the Israelites migrated to Egypt because they could not produce enough food in Canaan.

Those who had recently come from the Arabian Desert, however, found Canaan to be in truth a land "flowing with milk and honey." Food could not be produced there without effort, but when the population was willing to labor hard it usually was able to maintain itself. The Egyptian, Sinuhe, boasted about the figs, dates, and other products of Canaan.

Grains, vines, and olives were the basic agricultural products of ancient Canaan, as of other Mediterranean lands. Wheat, oats and barley were raised, along with beans, vetch, figs, pomegranates and nuts.

The cities of northern Phoenicia had an abundance of water flowing from the Lebanon mountains to the Mediterranean. To prevent erosion and to extend the amount of arable land, a system of terracing and irrigation was developed. In this way both summer and winter cultivation was possible to provide for the large population along the coast.

Terracing was not limited to Phoenicia, however. The mountainsides of Syria and Palestine were terraced by means of walls built a few yards apart to protect the soil and make farming possible. Vineyards, orchards, and gardens could be maintained in this way. Grains were raised with greater efficiency along the coastal plains and in the Esdraelon Valley.

In the excavations at Jericho, John Garstang and his associates unearthed storage jars containing wheat, barley, oats, millet, and lentils. We know that flax was raised at Jericho during the time of Joshua, for Rahab hid the Israelite spies on her roof and concealed them with "stalks of flax which she laid in order upon the roof" (Josh. 2:6). The "pottage" for which Esau exchanged his birthright (Gen. 25:29-34) was made of red lentils and water or milk. Other vegetables and meat or suet were sometimes added. Bread was dipped into the pot and used to convey the pottage to the mouth.

Reference is made to mandrakes (Gen. 30:14-18) which were gathered by Reuben at the time of wheat harvest and brought to his mother, Leah. The mandrake is a root, related to the potato and tomato, with a fruit resembling the plum. It grows wild and can be seen all over Palestine in May of each year.

W. F. Albright suggests that lettuce was grown in Palestine from the third and fourth millennium B.C. Egypt, Syria, and the Middle East in general also produced cucumbers at an early date (Num. 11:5; Isa. 1:8).

The instrument used for harvesting grain was the sickle which, before 2000 B.C., was made of flint teeth which were fastened with plaster into a bone or wooden handle. Later, iron was introduced. In the process of reaping, the harvester grasped a number of stalks with one hand, and with the other cut them off about a foot below the ears of grain. The remaining stubble was subsequently burned to fertilize the soil. The reapers were followed by binders who bound the grain into sheaves.

The so-called calendar, discovered during the excavations of Gezer by R. A. S. Macalister working with the British Palestine Exploration Fund (1902-08), describes the agricultural seasons of Palestine. Although the "calendar" probably should be dated about 925 B.C., the pattern of life it describes was doubtless pursued for centuries before that time:

> His two months are (olive) harvest,
> His two months are planting (grain),
> His two months are late planting;
> His month is hoeing up of flax,
> His month is harvest of barley
> His month is harvest and feasting;
> His two months are vine tending,
> His month is summer fruit.

5. The Cloth Industry

Spinning and weaving were carried on by the Canaanites during the third millennium before Christ. Archaeologists have discovered whorls of stone and of bone from this period. The industry was carried on in the home with wool as the earliest fabric. Canaanite wool is mentioned in the Nuzi documents (fifteenth century B.C.).

Flax grew in hot, low sections of Canaan such as the Jordan Plain near Jericho, where Scripture notes flax was used at the time of the conquest (Josh. 2:6). Loom weights used in making linen have been discovered at Teleilat el-Ghassul, northeast of the Dead Sea, dating back to the fourth millennium B.C.

6. The Alphabet

Chief among the debts which the West owe to the Canaanites is the alphabet. According to Greek tradition the art of writing was learned from a man named Cadmus. Actually Cadmus is but a Grecianized form of the Semitic word *Kedem,* which means "the East." The Greek word for *book, biblion,* from which our word "Bible" is derived, is the name of the Syrian city of Byblos, also known as Gebal.

Among the clay tablets discovered since 1929 at Ras Shamra, ancient Ugarit on the northern coast of Syria, were hundreds of documents dating from the fifteenth and fourteenth centuries B.C. written in a cuneiform alphabet which had not been previously known. The cuneiform used by the Sumerians, Babylonians and Assyrians was a cumbersome means of writing in which hundreds of syllables were represented by as many combinations of wedges. The alphabet at Ugarit comprised thirty-one alphabetic signs which were used in the production of a variety of literary and business documents.

By 1200 B.C. when the Canaanites felt pressure from the Philistines who had settled along the southern coastal plain and from the Israelites who had invaded the land from the east and conquered much of the interior hill country, the Canaanites were largely confined to the coastal territories north of Mount Carmel known as Phoenicia. From Tyre and Sidon, the great Phoenician cities, traders and colonists sailed to the islands of the Mediterranean and northern Africa. It was from contacts with these Phoenicians that the alphabet was introduced into Greece.

8

AN EPISODE IN WORLD POLITICS

The patriarchal records place the focus of attention upon a man, Abraham, and the providence of God by which a sovereign purpose was fulfilled through his descendants, Isaac and Jacob. Although mention is made of surrounding peoples, we look to extra-Biblical sources to gain information concerning their history.

On one occasion, however, Abraham became involved in the politics of the Fertile Crescent. In that instance, described in Genesis 14, Abraham was called upon to rescue his nephew Lot, who had been taken captive by a confederation of kings from the East.

Four kings from Mesopotamia had demanded tribute of the city-states of Canaan. The eastern kings are mentioned by name: Amraphel, king of Shinar; Chedorlaomer, king of Elam; Arioch, king of Ellasar; and Tidal, king of Goiim (or "nations"). The leader of the confederacy appears to be the Elamite, Chedorlaomer (Gen. 14:4). The name of this king is authentically Elamite and we know that, during the Patriarchal Age, Elamites controlled a large area. About 1950 B.C., Elamites conquered the city of Ur, once the center of a thriving Sumerian civilization. The kings of Elam desired to control the whole of Sumer and, about 1770 B.C. the Elamite ruler Kudur-mabuk conquered the important state of Larsa.

The name of "Amraphel, king of Shinar," was once popularly identified with the great Babylonian lawgiver, Hammurabi (*ca.* 1728-1686 B.C.), but this is ruled out by both linguistic and chronological considerations. The name, however, is Semitic, as we would expect of a king of Babylon. Several Mesopotamian kings bore the name Arriwuk ("Arioch"), a fact known from the Mari tablets. We do not know the identity of the state which he ruled, although Ellasar may be a variant of Larsa. Several Hittite kings bore the name Tudhalias, which may be the Biblical "Tidal king of Nations." The "nations" may have been a confederacy, the nature of which is unknown to us.

The eastern kings fought and rendered tributary the kings of Sodom, Gomorrah, Admah, and Zeboiim in the Valley of Siddim, the southern portion of what is now the Dead Sea. This area subsequently was submerged as a result of a cataclysmic judgment (Gen. 19).

We are told that the Canaanite kings from the Dead Sea area paid their tribute faithfully for twelve years. In the thirteenth year they rebelled, but it was evidently too late in the season for the eastern alliance to do anything about it. The following year, however, Chedorlaomer and his allies marched west.

The eastern confederates followed the route of the Fertile Crescent into northern Syria. They probably marched through Damascus and then took the main road through eastern Palestine. The towns of Ashteroth-karnaim, Ham, and Shaveh-kiriathaim were inhabited by Rephaim, Zuzim, and Emim, aboriginal inhabitants of Canaan who lost their tribal identity before the time of the Israelite conquest. The east-Jordan country was explored by Nelson Glueck, who concluded that there were large cities in the region during the time of Abraham, but that it was largely uninhabited for about four centuries beginning about 1700 B.C.

Chedorlaomer journed southward as far as to El-paran, probably the ancient name of Ezion-geber at the head of the Gulf of Aqabah. In the southern part of the country the eastern confederacy defeated the Horites, or Hurrians who had settled at Mount Seir (Edom). On the northward march they went to En Mishpat – Kadesh, in the Amalekite country southeast of Beer-sheba, and then to Hazezon-tamar (En-gedi) which was occupied by Amorites.

The king of Sodom and his allies fought Chedorlaomer in the Valley of Siddim, with disastrous results. In their flight some of the men of Sodom and Gomorrah fell into the slime pits, while others escaped to the mountains. The enemy was able to take as booty all of the property which had to be left behind, and a number of men, including Lot.

One of the men who had escaped alive brought word of the defeat of the men of Sodom and the capture of Lot to Abraham. The patriarch then gathered his personal army of three hundred eighteen men and pursued the enemy to Dan, later to become the northern frontier of Israel, and then, after defeating them in battle, followed them to Hobah, north of Damascus. Abraham was able to rescue Lot and those who were with him along with the property of the men of Sodom which had been taken.

The "kings" involved in these battles were rulers of city-states, rather than "kings" in the later sense of the term. The fact that Abraham was able to defeat them is still no mean achievement. He probably harassed them by repeated attacks and retreats until they were weakened. Then he made the final thrust which liberated Lot and his companions.

Abraham and the other patriarchs attempted to live in peace with the peoples of Canaan. It was only through the attempt of Lot to make common cause with the men of Sodom that Abraham became involved in this bit of international politics.

9

THE RELIGION OF THE CANAANITES

The pernicious effect of Canaanite religion on Israel was not felt until the days of the judges (cf. Judg. 2:11-13), but it became one of the greatest sources of temptation to the covenant people in the years between the conquest of Canaan and the Babylonian exile.

The reader of the Old Testament is familiar with Baal, the infamous "high places," and other aspects of a religion which was constantly denounced by the prophets of the God of Israel. Further clues to the nature of Canaanite religion were gathered from the writings of the ancient Egyptians, Phoenician records, and Greek literature. The latter were, at best, fragmentary, and frequently far removed from the historical situation in which Baalism was a vital force. Discoveries made since 1929 at Ras Shamra, however, have completely changed the picture. Ras Shamra, ancient Ugarit, is a small Arab village near modern Latakia, opposite the "point" of the island of Cyprus. The site was probably occupied since the first settlements of man in Syria. The lowest level of the mound is believed to date from the fifth millennium B.C. It is thought that Amorites and Semitic Canaanites pushed northward from the Arabian Desert and settled in the area during the third millennium B.C., bringing about important ethnic changes in Ugarit. Early in the second millennium an alliance was made with Egypt. Discoveries at Ugarit have shown strong Egyptian influences along with artifacts from the Minoan, Cretan civilization during this period.

During the heyday of Ugaritic prosperity — the fifteenth and fourteenth centuries B.C. — the poetic epics and myths of the ancient Canaanites were recorded on clay tablets in a cuneiform script. The Ugaritic alphabet is one of the earliest known to man. Our interest in the tablets arises from the relatively complete picture they present of Canaanite religion. We are no longer dependent on second hand accounts of the creed and cult of the Canaanites. Those who worshiped Baal and his associates have left us a first hand witness to their faith.

The nominal head of the Canaanite pantheon was El, a "remote, high god," who interfered little in the affairs of the world. El may be thought of as a mild old gentleman who delegated authority to his children, only reserving the right to be final arbiter in the event of disputes among them.

In a slightly different form, the word Il, or Ilu is the Akkadian word for "god." The cuneiform sign *il* is regularly prefixed to signs representing the popular deities of the Akkadian Semitic world. We read, then, of "the god Ishtar," "the god Ea," and "the god Baal." In this sense, *il* is the equivalent of our "god."

Just as we have one word for God or the gods, so the Hebrew Elohim served a dual purpose. It may speak of God, creator of heaven and earth (Gen. 1:1). When, however, Jacob asked his family to "put away the strange gods" which were in their midst (Gen. 35:2), or the rebellious Israelites asked Aaron to make gods to lead them from Sinai (Exod. 32:1), Elohim is also used. Depending on its context, Elohim in the Bible may refer to the God of Israel, or the gods of the surrounding nations. Similarly El, or Il in the ancient Near East may be a distinct personal being – the El of Ugaritic mythology – or simply a generic term for deity. The fact that El was the father of the gods may account for their bearing his "name."

El, in the Canaanite mythology, presided over the assembly of the gods who gathered in the farthermost reaches of the north. The north, Mount Saphon, was an area concerning which little was known by the ancient Semites, and it became to them what Mount Olympus became to the Greeks.

The consort of El in the Ugaritic texts was named Asherat, "Lady of the Sea." In the form Asherah, the name appears about forty times in the Old Testament, especially in the books of Kings and Chronicles. In Ugarit the name Elat ("the goddess" – a feminine form of El) is also used of Asherat.

When not the name of a goddess, the term Asherah, and its plural, Asherim, denote the wooden poles which stood at Canaanite places of worship. In the Authorized Version of the Bible the word is regularly translated "grove." The terms "sacred tree" or "Asherah image" would better convey the thought of the original. The Asherah is thought to have been the trunk of a tree with the branches chopped off. It was erected beside the altar of Baal (Judg. 6:25, 28) in the fertility cult which was scathingly denounced by the Israelite prophets.

El and his wife Asherah produced a family of seventy Elim, gods and goddesses, best known of whom was Baal (meaning "master," "lord"), who was identified with the storm god, Hadad. Baal was the god of fertility responsible for the germination and growth of crops, the increase of flocks and herds, and the fecundity of human families.

Baal worship was the most degrading aspect of Canaanite civilization. Devotees brought wine, oil, first fruits, and firstlings of the flocks to the "high places." Near the rock altar was a *mazzebah* or sacred pillar which represented the male element in the fertility cult, corresponding to the Asherah, or female element. Chambers were maintained for sacred prostitution by *kedeshim* ("male prostitutes") and *kedeshoth* ("sacred harlots") (cf. I Kings 14:23, 24; II Kings 23:7). It should be noted that the language of the prophets who describe unfaithfulness to the Lord as adultery, and speak of those who forget the God of Israel as going "whoring after idols," is more than figure of speech.

We first read of the appeal of Baalism to Israel before Joshua brought his people into Canaan. Numbers 22 records an incident in which a Babylonian soothsayer named Balaam played the principal role. Balak of Moab was frightened at reports of the defeat of powerful Amorite kings at the hands of Israel. In concert with the elders of Midian he sent for Balaam, trusting that he could pronounce a potent curse on Israel and thus insure its defeat. Unable to do this, Balaam devised a fiendish plan. He proposed that the Midianites invite the Israelites to the worship of Baal at Peor, knowing that this would mean apostasy from the God of Israel. The Hebrew historian writes:

> And Israel abode at Shittim, and the people began to commit harlotry with the daughters of Moab. And they called the people unto the sacrifices of their gods; and the people did eat and bowed down to their gods. And Israel joined himself unto the Baal of Peor; and the anger of the Lord was kindled against Israel. (Num. 25:1-3).

It has been suggested that the term "joined himself," related to the noun *tsemed,* "a couple," "a pair," might be rendered, "they paired off" — an Israelite and a Moabitess — in the worship of the Baal of Mount Peor.

While Baal, "rider of the clouds," is in essence one god, at the sound of whose voice the mountains rock, the earth shakes, and all his enemies flee in terror, in actual cult he is identified with each locality in which he is worshiped. In addition to the

Baal of Peor we read of Baal-gad (Josh. 11:17), Baal-hazor (II Sam. 13:23), Baal-zephon (Num. 33:7) and others. The New Testament mentions Beelzebul (Matt. 12:24 R.S.V., a variant of Beel-zebub), a name which may be associated with Baal-zebul of the Ugaritic texts. In Ugarit Baal-zebul signifies "Prince Baal," and was a term of high honor. The gods of the heathen were regarded as evil spirits by the Biblical writers, and Beel-zebub or Beel-zebul became a name for Satan.

Baal-zebub was the name of the god of Ekron, according to II Kings 1:2, 3, 6, 16. The original may have been Baal-zebul, which was changed in contempt by the Israelites who considered a name meaning "Lord of flies" more fitting. The name of Saul's son Esh-baal (I Chron. 8:33), meaning "man of Baal," was changed to Ish-bosheth, "man of shame" (II Sam. 3:14). Similarly Jonathan's son Mephibosheth (II Sam. 4:4) is also named Merib-baal (I Chron. 8:34). Equating Baal with shame, the author of Kings felt justified in changing "Baal" names in order to eliminate a reference to religious ideas which had proved a stumbling-block to Israel for so many years. Saul and Jonathan, in giving their sons "Baal" names doubtless used the term as a synonym for Israel's God, their true "Lord," or "Master." The word, however, while having an innocent use, later was so associated with the evils of Canaanite Baalism that it was deemed obnoxious for a loyal Israelite.

The sister and spouse of Baal in the Ugaritic texts is known as Anat. Although bearing the epithet "the virgin," Anat was the goddess of passion, destructive as well as positive. Love and fertility were her domain, although Baal himself occupied the leading role in the cult. The lewd side of Anat worship may be noted from the figurines and pottery plaques of the nude Anat which have been dug from various Palestinian sites dating to the second millennium B.C.

Anat is goddess of war as well as sex. She fights Baal's enemies, smiting them and wading in their blood, even washing her hands in it! She attacked Mot, the god of death, and forced him to give back her brother, Baal. She cleaved Mot with her sword, ground him up and planted him in the ground.

The goddess Anat may appear in the name of the Israelite judge Shamgar, ben (son of) Anat(h). Either Anat(h) is the name of a parent of Shamgar, a fact which would be consistent with the religious syncretism of those days, or it may simply mean "warrior" – i.e. a "son" of the goddess of war! Anat may also be identified with the "queen of heaven" to whom Jews of

Jeremiah's time burned incense (Jer. 44:19). We cannot be positive about such identifications, however, because the three principal Canaanite, goddesses are constantly confused and it is often impossible to identify the activities of a goddess unless she is specifically named.

Like Asherah and Anat, Astarte (Ashtaroth) was primarily concerned with sex. According to Philo, the Phoenicians attributed to Astarte two sons, Pothos ("sexual desire") and Eros ("sexual love"). In Egypt, Anat and Astarte were fused into one goddess, Antart. Theodore Gaster suggests that the three goddesses represent three aspects of womanhood:

> Ashterah was the wife and mother, sedate and matronly mistress of the home and female head of the family. Ashtarth (Astarte) was the sweetheart and mistress, a glamorous and voluptuous embodiment of sexual passion and therefore also the genius of reproduction and of fecundity in general. Anath was the young girl, a beautiful and virginal creature, full of youthful zest and vigor and addicted especially to the thrills of battle and the excitement of the chase. Since, however, all of them were *au fond* but aspects of the same thing, they naturally shared several qualities and attributes in common, and were not infrequently confused with one another.[1]

The Canaanite pantheon included a host of deities which served as the deification of natural phenomena. Shemesh, the sun, received considerable attention. Four towns in Scripture bear the name Beth-shemesh, and there is another named En-Shemesh. Such names indicate that the town was devoted to the worship of the deity whose name it bears. The Israelites, of course, occupied towns which had been settled by earlier Canaanites, and the names continued in use.

Jericho is named for Yareah, the moon god, as is Beth-yerah south of Tiberias. Under another name, Sin, the moon god had been worshiped in Ur and Haran at the time of Abraham.

Sedeq, "right," and Mishor, "equity," were attendants of the sun god who, because he surveys all things, was also regarded as a god of justice. Dawn and sunset were deified in the persons of Shahar and Shalem, "the celestial ones," who have been equated with Castor and Pollux of Greek and Roman mythology.

One of the Ugaritic texts speaks of an offering to "Queen Shapash (the sun) and to the stars." Shapash was a feminine manifestation, at Ugarit, of Shemesh, or Shamash, the sun god. Another text speaks of "the army of the sun and the host of the day," in connection with a ceremony performed on a rooftop. In the days preceding the captivity of Judah, Jeremiah com-

---

1. Theodore Gaster, "The Religion of the Canaanites," *Forgotten Religions* V. Ferm, ed., p. 125.

plained, "because of all the houses upon whose roofs they have burned incense unto all the host of heaven . . ." (Jer. 19:13).

Dagon of the Old Testament finds his counterpart in the Ugaritic Dagan, the god of grain and the genius of the crops. He was worshiped by the Philistines who built temples to him at Gaza and Ashdod (Judg. 16:23-30; I Sam. 5:1-7). Following the battle of Mount Gilboa, during which Saul and Jonathan died, the Philistines took the head of Saul and fastened it "in the temple of Dagan" at Beth-shan (I Chron. 10:10). At least two Beth-Dagons are known — one in the lowlands of Judah near the Philistine border (Josh. 15:33, 41), and another in Asher on the frontier toward Zebulon, near Mount Carmel.

The divine smith of the Canaanite pantheon was Koshar (or Kauthar) who also bore the name Hasis. Gaster translates the compound name, "Sir Adroit and Cunning." Koshar is the craftsman and inventor of tools and weapons. He finds his counterpart in the Egyptian Ptah, and the classical Hephaestus and Vulcan. Koshar was also the discoverer and patron of music. Philo of Byblos considers him (under the name Chusor) the originator of magical incantations. The Book of Genesis, by contrast, traces the arts and crafts to human origins. Jubal, a son of Lamech and Adah "was the father of all such as handle the harp and pipe." Tubal-cain, son of Lamech and Zillah was "the forger of every cutting instrument of brass and iron" (Gen. 4:21-22).

The nether world and the barren places of earth were the realm of Mot (the Canaanite god of death). Mot is the particular enemy of Baal, and the fertility cult in general, as death is the enemy of life. In his manifestation as Resheph, "the ravager," he is the god of plague and pestilence. One of the Karatepe inscriptions (8th century B.C.) calls him "Resheph of Birds," perhaps alluding to vulture-like characteristics. Mot also appears of Horon, "He of the Pit." The Book of Joshua (10:8-11) mentions a Beth-horon in the valley of Aijalon.

The sea was controlled by Yam, another enemy of Baal. "Prince Sea," as Gaster calls him, contended with Baal for mastery over the earth. Yam also appears under the name Lotan, the seven-headed monster of the deep. The name appears in the Old Testament as Leviathan. The Psalmist praises God for His power:

> Thou didst shatter the heads of the sea-monsters in the waters. Thou didst crush the heads of Leviathan. (Psalm 74:13-14).

The Biblical writers did not, of course, accept the Canaanite mythology. They were prepared, as pious Israelites, to fight it to the death. Poetic forms and figures of speech, however, were used as a means of expressing the power of the God of Israel. Writing before the discovery of the Ugaritic texts, John Davis said, "Leviathan may be merely a creation of the popular fancy, an imaginary sea monster; the inspired poets and prophets of Israel subsidizing fable to serve in the illustration of truth."[2]

Molech or Milcom is mentioned in Scripture as the national God of Ammon (I Kings 11:5, 33). In the third millennium before Christ, the god Malik appears in the Assyro-Babylonian pantheon. The excavations at Mari on the middle Euphrates show that Muluk was worshiped in that region around 1800 B.C. In II Kings 17:31 we are told that the gods of the area of Sepharvaim – from which the Assyrians transplanted colonists to replace the men of Israel who had been taken into captivity – were named Adrammelech and Anammelech. The Tyrians worshiped Melkarth – the Melk (king) of the city.

Molech worship was expressly forbidden in the Mosaic law (Lev. 18:21; 20:1-5). Nevertheless it was popularly observed in times of apostasy. Solomon built an altar to Molech in the Valley of Hinnom at Tophet (I Kings 11:7). Both Ahaz and Manasseh offered their sons in sacrifice to Molech (II Kings 16:3; 21:6). Josiah, in his attempt to establish the Law of the Lord, desecrated the Hinnom Molech center in order to render it useless for pagan religious practices (II Kings 23:10). The Molech cult was revived, however, and the prophecies of Jeremiah and Ezekiel afford evidence that it continued to the time of the Exile (Jer. 7:29-34; Ezek. 16:20-21; 20:26, 31; 23:37-39).

The term Molech is related to the Semitic word for king (Hebrew *melech*). It originally signified a counsellor. Its meaning is not far removed from Baal, "master." The Palmyrenes had a deity whom they worshiped as Malach-baal. Milch-baal is a Phoenician personal name, and it is certain that the Baal whom Elijah challenged was the Baal of Tyre, otherwise known as Melcharth.

According to Albright, the concept of *Mulku,* or kingship, gave rise to the concept of *mulkana* which means "promise" in Syriac. The deity Molech became the god of vows and solemn promises, and children were sacrificed to him as the harshest and most binding pledge of the sanctity of a promise.

---

2. John Davis, *A Dictionary of the Bible,* pp. 449-50.

Molech worship included a practice which is described in Scripture as making a son or daughter pass through the fire. Some scholars have thought of this as a harmless rite of purification from which the child emerged unscathed. The testimony of Scripture, however, indicates that the child died as a result of this hideous rite. Ezekiel complains, "... thou hast taken thy sons and thy daughters ... and these hast thou sacrificed ... to be devoured ... thou hast slain my children and delivered them to cause them to pass through the fire" (Ezek. 16:20-21. cf 23:37). The evidence is clear that children were slaughtered and burnt like other sacrificial victims. Josephus says of Ahaz, "He also sacrificed his own son as a burnt offering to the idols according to the custom of the Canaanites." Archaeologists have found hundreds of urns containing the bones of children of from four to twelve years of age who had been burned alive.

The Greek writers who touched upon the subject of the history and customs of the Phoenicians and their colonies note with disgust the practice of child sacrifice. It was an established and prominent part of the religion of Carthage to burn children in a pit of fire. Albertus Pieters observes:

> It is interesting to note the statement in Josephus that the grand niece of Jezebel, about 20 years after the death of Jezebel's father, founded the city of Carthage in Northern Africa, the forces of which, under Hannibal, nearly overwhelmed Rome.... Had Jezebel succeeded in Palestine and Hannibal in Italy, this faith might have overspread the world. The sword of Scipio Africanus and the faith of Elijah the Tishbite were strange allies, but the Lord used them both to save the world from such a fate.[3]

It is known that human sacrifices were offered by the Phoenicians during times of calamity, although there is no specific reference to them in Tyre itself. The annual Melkart festival at Tyre had much in common with Baal worship in other Canaanite communities. When the prolonged heat of the summer would burn everything up, Melkarth would offer himself a sacrifice to the sun in order to win the favor of heaven. During the month Peritius (February-March) the festival of the awakening, or resurrection of Melkarth was observed. Elijah's comment, "Cry aloud ... peradventure he is sleeping and must be awaked" (I Kings 18:27) may be a reference to this belief.

Classified as a mystery cult by modern students of religion is the worship of Adonis, which became popular in Hellenistic times. Adonis was the son of Cinyras, mythical king of Byblos. He was the husband of Astarte or Ashtoreth. The legend relates that Adonis was hunting wild boar in the Lebanon mountains

3. Albertus Pieters, *Notes on Old Testament History,* p. 97.

when the animal which he was pursuing turned upon him and so gored his thigh that he died of the wound. From that time on he was mourned annually. At the time of the summer solstice, the anniversary of his death, all of the women of Byblos went in a wild procession to Aphaea in the Lebanon where his temple stood. There they wept and wailed on account of his death. The river which his blood had once stained turned red to show its sympathy with the mourners, and was thought to flow with his blood afresh. After the weeping had continued for a definite time, an image of the god was buried in the sacred temple precinct, bringing the mourning to an end. On the next day Adonis was supposed to return to life. His image was disinterred and carried back to the temple with music and dances. Wild orgies accompanied the rejoicing. Adonis at Byblos was the Phoenician counterpart of Tammuz, or Dumuzi, the Babylonian god of pasture and flocks, whose worship had reached Jerusalem (Ezek. 8:14). In the Babylonian epics, Tammuz dies in the autumn, when vegetation withers, departs to the underworld, and is recovered by the mourning Ishtar in time to return in the springtime to the fertilized upper-world.

Cyrus H. Gordon, observing that Baal is god of dew as well as rain, asserts that there is no Canaanite seasonal pattern wherein Baal spends part of each year in the netherworld.[4] He sees, rather, a pattern in which years of plenty are followed by a year or more of famine. It is during the time of drought that Baal is presumed to be in the clutches of Mot (death). In either instance, however, the Biblical record stands out in marked contrast to the mythological interpretation of fertility which characterized the thought of ancient Canaan.

4. Cyrus H. Gordon, "Canaanite Mythology," in *Mythologies of the Ancient World,* edited by Samuel N. Kramer, pp. 183-217.

10

THE DAILY LIVES OF THE PATRIARCHS

Although the patriarchs are described as tent-dwellers, Scripture also makes it clear that Abraham had come from a city, Ur of the Chaldees in the Hebrew text of Genesis 11:31. Cyrus H. Gordon has suggested that Abraham was actually a merchant trader from a city of nothern Mesopotamia named Ura.[1] The merchants of Ura are known to have engaged in trade with Ugarit, along the Mediterranean coast.

When the Shechemites sought to form an alliance with the Israelites, they mentioned trade as part of the alliance terms: "You shall dwell with us, and the land shall be open to you; dwell and trade in it, and get property in it" (Gen. 24:10). Similarly Joseph, while testing the brothers who had sold him into slavery, asked them to bring Benjamin to him in Egypt, adding "then I shall know that you are not spies but honest men, and I will deliver to you your brother [i.e. Simeon], and you shall trade in the land" (Gen. 42:34).

Gordon summarizes the life of Abraham as follows: "Abraham comes from beyond the Euphrates, plies his trade in Canaan, visits Egypt, deals with Hittites, makes treaties with Philistines, forms military alliances with Amorites, fights kinglets from as far off as Elam, marries the Egyptian Hagar, etc. His contacts and freedom of movement reflect a sophisticated milieu where an international order . . . made such a career and such enterprise possible."

The patriarchs lived in tents, or "houses of hair" as they are called by desert Bedouin today. Goat's hair was hand-woven by the women into a very satisfactory cloth. Narrow strips were made on small looms, and then sewn together. Following the

1. Cyrus H. Gordon, "Abraham and the Merchants of Ura," *Journal of Near Eastern Studies,* XVII, 1, p. 30.

time of the shearing of the goats, old tents might be patched and new tents set up.

Tents varied in size, depending upon the number of people they were designed to accommodate. An average tent might cover a ten by fifteen foot area. It would be supported by nine poles, arranged in three rows. The middle row might be seven feet high, and the outer rows only six feet, creating a slope from the center.

The inside of the tent was divided into two compartments. The one used by the men served also as a reception room for guests. An inner room, used as the women's apartment, served also as a storage room for cooking pots and other utensils.

A wealthy family might have several tents. This would be of particular advantage in a family with more than one wife. It was probably from the seclusion of her own tent that Sarah heard the incredible report that she would bear a son in her old age (Gen. 18:10). When Isaac married Rebekah, the young lady who had come from Paddan-aram to be his bride, he took her into the tent of Sarah, his deceased mother (Gen. 24:67). Jacob seems to have had a large number of tents for his wives and servants. When Laban had overtaken Jacob seeking the idols which Rachel had stolen we read, "So Laban went into Jacob's tent, and into Leah's tent, and into the tent of the two maidservants, but he did not find them" (Gen. 31:33).

The interior of the tent had very simple furnishings. The soil itself was the floor of the tent. A few straw mats or woolen rugs would imply a degree of luxury. A sheet of metal or a few stones set up at the tent door would serve as a stove for cooking the daily supply of bread. Necessary items for preparing and storing food would include earthen vessels and goat-skin bottles for water, wine, and milk. When Abraham dismissed Hagar and Ishmael he, "rose early in the morning, and took bread and a skin of water, and gave it to Hagar" (Gen. 21:14).

During the day most of the activities of the household were conducted at the door of the tent. Abraham is depicted as sitting "at the door of his tent in the heat of the day" (Gen. 18:1) when three strangers approached. With characteristic Bedouin hospitality he ordered that water be brought to wash their feet and suggested that they rest under a nearby tree. Then the patriarch entered Sarah's tent, asking her to "Make ready, quickly, three measures of fine meal, knead it, and make cakes" (Gen. 18:6). He next chose a calf from the herd, and ordered a servant to prepare it. Abraham also took curds and milk and gave a hearty meal to his visitors (Gen. 18:1-8).

Milk was an important article in the diet of the patriarchs. We read of the milk of cows, sheep (Deut. 32:14), goats (Prov. 27:27), and camels (Gen. 32:15). The milk of camels is rich and strong, but not very sweet. It is prized today among nomadic Arabs.

The word which the Revised Standard Version renders "curds" in Genesis 18:8, has been traditionally translated "butter." Scripture usage, however, makes it clear that curdled milk is meant. This is still considered a delicacy among the Arabs. Milk is poured into a skin bottle which still contains sour clots from the previous milking. It is then shaken, and the result is the beverage which is known in Hebrew as *ḥem'ah,* "curds."

In addition to the meat of the calf which Abraham prepared for his guests, the patriarchs ate bullocks, lambs, kids (Gen. 27:8-9), and the flesh of game animals (Gen. 25:28). These might be boiled, roasted on hot stoves, or made into a stew. The food was served in the containers in which it was cooked.

The fruits of the land – figs, grapes, and dates – formed staple articles of diet in patriarchal times as they did later. Honey was also regarded as a delicacy, and it was so plentiful that Canaan was called the land "flowing with milk and honey" (Exod. 3:8). Honey was produced by bees from fruits and flowers and placed in the cells of a comb (cf. Psalm 19:10). Wild honey might be found in rocks (Deut. 32:13), in trees (I Sam. 14:25) and even in the carcass of an animal (Judg. 14:8). The term honey (Arabic *dibs*) is applied not only to the product of bees, but also to a man-made syrup produced from dates and grapes. Honey in both forms took the place of sugar (cf. Exod. 16:31).

When Jacob wished to send "the choice fruits of the land" to Egypt, we read that he gave to his sons, "a little balm and a little honey, gum, myrrh, pistachio nuts, and almonds" (Gen. 43:11). These were "luxury items" sent to Egypt in the hope that the rulers there would provide much needed grain for famine-stricken Canaan.

Although the patriarchs moved about the land of Canaan, the Scripture records make it clear that they practiced agriculture or, at least, maintained close relations with those who did. Bread ("cakes") was an essential item in the diet of the patriarchs (Gen. 19:3; 21:14; 27:17). As a matter of fact the patriarchs spent considerable periods of time in several of the places where they settled. Jacob is pictured as settled in the Hebron area at the time his sons pasture the flocks as far away as Shechem and Dothan (Gen. 37:12-17). Isaac sojourned in Gerar long enough to sow his seed and reap the harvest (Gen. 26:12). It was lack of grain that forced Jacob to send his sons to Egypt (Gen. 42:1-2).

Small quantities of grain could be prepared by the use of a pestle in a stone mortar (Lev. 2:14). For larger amounts, a mill was made, consisting of two circular stones, the upper of which could be rotated by hand while the lower remained stationary. This process produced the fine flour which was prized by the conscientious host (cf. Gen. 18:6). To make unleavened bread the flour was mixed with water and salt in a wooden kneading bowl (Exod. 8:3; 12:34).

The dough was formed into flat cakes, twelve to sixteen inches in diameter and one-eighth to one-quarter inch thick. To bake the bread a fire was built on a flat stone. When the stone was heated, the embers were raked off and the cake placed on the stone and covered with the embers and ashes. When one side was baked, the cake was turned over and the process repeated (cf. Hosea 7:8). Leavened bread was made by adding to the dough a lump saved from the previous baking. Many nomads carry a metal plate for baking which is placed over a fire built in a hole in the ground or over a fireplace in the corner of the tent.

For centuries the dress of the patriarchs was largely a matter of conjecture based upon the attire of nomadic Arabs who were observed in Bible lands in recent centuries. It was inferred that, since life in the East had not drastically changed over many centuries, Abraham probably looked very much like a modern sheikh of the desert.

Archaeology sometimes confirms the truthfulness of traditional ideas, and sometimes it gives them a rude jolt. The latter has been true of the concepts of dress during partriarchal times. We now have an actual painting, in color, from the tomb of an Egyptian nobleman at Beni Hasan, depicting a nomadic chieftain from Palestine with his retinue. It is dated during the nineteenth century B.C. and gives us an authentic picture of the way in which Canaanites dressed during patriarchal times.

Egyptians in the painting are wearing white linen loincloths, but the Asiastics are clothed in ornate embroidered garments. A number of the men wear striped skirts which reach from the waist to the knee. Other men, and all of the women wear a single piece garment, fastened at one shoulder, which reaches well below the knee. A little boy wears red shorts. The men wear sandals, but the women have a more substantial "boot." The clothing is made of wool which has been woven in many colors.

The men in the painting are bearded, and most of them have throw-sticks or javelins. One has a bow and arrow and one, interestingly, a lyre (the Biblical "harp"). On a donkey they carry two pairs of goat-skin bellows which indicates that these traders also did metal work. A water-skin is on the back of the man playing the lyre.

The women have long hair and are clustered together. They are close to the children, two of whom are riding a donkey and one following behind.

11

SOCIAL AND BUSINESS LIFE IN PATRIARCHAL TIMES

Our most detailed description of life during patriarchal times comes from the city of Nuzi, or Nuzu, southeast of Nineveh. Clay tablets discovered there were written by Hurrian scribes in the Akkadian language about 1500 B.C. They reflect patterns of life which were characteristic of northeastern Mesopotamia during the period when the patriarchs and members of their families lived in Haran and the Paddan-aram area.

A large number of Nuzi documents deal with adoption. As in Israel, land could not be permanently alienated at Nuzi. A legal fiction could be devised, however, so that a man with money and insufficient land could be adopted by a man with land who needed money. Through the fiction of adoption, land could be transferred within the new "family." One Nuzi family amassed an enormous estate by means of these fictitious adoptions.

There were, of course, real adoptions at Nuzi. A childless family might adopt a son to insure the continuity of the family. The adopted son would show filial respect to his new parents during their lifetime, and care for the funeral rites at the time of their death. Adoption tablets carefully outline the duties and responsibilities of each party to the contract.

On occasion the Nuzi tablets mention the adoption of a beloved family servant, or slave. Such seems to have been the relationship between Abraham and Eliezer who apparently was "the elder of his house that ruled over all that he had" (Gen. 24:2). God made it clear to Abraham, however, that his heir would be a natural son, and not the servant Eliezer.

Adoption contracts usually provided for the possibility of the birth of a natural son into the family. In such cases the adopted son took a subordinate position to the natural son. After the birth of Ishmael, Eliezer would lose his priority in Abraham's family.

The conduct of Sarah in urging her husband to have sexual relations with Hagar (Gen. 16:2) is inexplicable by modern standards. The Nuzi tablets make it clear, however, that this was not true in ancient Mesopotamia. The prime purpose of marriage, at least from the legal point of view, was the procreation of children, and marriage contracts specified that a wife who did not provide her husband with offspring was obligated to provide a handmaid who would be able to do so. The position of the wife was often protected by a provision in the contract which stated that the handmaid was to continue as her slave. This provision was also part of the law code of Hammurabi of Babylon. The handmaid and her child were also protected, however. The lawful wife had no right to dismiss them from her household. After Hagar knew that she had conceived a child of Abraham, she showed a spirit of contempt for her mistress, but she was still reckoned the handmaid of Sarah (Gen. 16:6). Being harshly treated she fled from Sarah and headed toward Shur (a word meaning "wall," which probably refers to the wall which had been built by the Egyptians at the frontier of their country to keep out the Asiatic Bedouins). The Angel of the Lord met Hagar by a well and urged her to return home and submit herself to her mistress, Sarah. She did so, and in due time Ishmael was born and became Abraham's heir. God, however, appeared to Abraham and assured the patriarch that he would have a son by Sarah, his wife (Gen. 17:15-19). Ishmael, the prophecy stated, would become a great people, but the covenant blessing would continue through the line of Isaac (Gen. 17:20-21), the son who would be born to Sarah. After the birth of Isaac, Sarah wanted to expel Ishmael and his mother (Gen. 21:9, 10), but Abraham was grieved at the thought and only complied with his wife's request when God gave him a direct command to do so (Gen. 21:12).

That Sarah's action in providing Hagar as a handmaid for Abraham is not unusual in patriarchal times is clear from the subsequent conduct of Rachel and Leah. Unable to bear children herself, the beautiful Rachel suggested that Jacob have children by Bilhah, her maid (Gen. 29:3). In fact the children of Jacob (Israel) trace their ancestry to four mothers: Leah, Rachel (who subsequently bore two sons), and the two maids, Bilhah and Zilpah. Preference was shown to the sons of wives rather than handmaids. One of the prime causes of factions among Jacob's sons was the fact that they had different mothers. Joseph and Benjamin, the children of the beloved Rachel, were always their father's favorites.

The relations between Jacob and Laban are also illustrated in the Nuzi tablets. At the time when Jacob arrived at Paddan-aram, Laban does not appear to have had any sons of his own. A man with daughters, but no sons, frequently adopted his son-in-law, who would assume filial obligations and become heir to the property of his wife's father. Laban appears to have adopted Jacob who had married his two daughters, Leah and Rachel. Later, however, we read of sons in the household of Laban, a fact which would remove Jacob from the favored position. When friction arose, Jacob, who had been cheated by Laban several times, determined to return to Canaan with his wives and property. While preparing to leave, Rachel, without Jacob's knowledge, stole the *teraphim*, or family idols, of Laban's household (Gen. 31:19, 34, 35). When he learned what had happened, Laban pursued the caravan indignantly asking, "Wherefore hast thou stolen my gods?" (Gen. 31:30). The significance of these "gods," or *teraphim*, is illustrated in the Nuzi tablets. They were not only regarded as "good luck" charms, but they also insured to their possessor rights to the family inheritance. Rachel, evidently, determined to secure for her husband the right to be Laban's chief heir in place of her brothers who would normally have taken the *teraphim*.

Inheritance was subject to transfer within the family at Nuzi. We read of a man who transferred a grove which he had inherited to his brother in return for three sheep. This forms a striking parallel to the conduct of Esau and Jacob. When hungry Jacob exclaimed, "Give me, I pray thee, some of that red pottage to eat . . . ," Jacob countered by demanding, "Sell me first thy birthright" (Gen. 25:30-34). Considering his birthright of little value, Esau exchanged it for the "mess of pottage" (cf. Heb. 12:16).

We also learn that oral blessings were considered binding in the courts at Nuzi. The sanctity of the word was highly regarded among the Israelites, who honored their word even when they were tricked into making pronouncements contrary to their real intent. After Jacob succeeded in fooling his father about his true identity, Isaac gave him the blessing intended for Esau. When the truth was learned, Isaac realized that he had given his blessing and would not go back on his word (Gen. 27:23). At a later time, Joshua honored his covenant with the Gibeonites even though he had been fooled by them into thinking that they had come from a distant land (Josh. 9). Court proceedings from Nuzi contain the record of an oral blessing similar to those pronounced by Jacob as he gathered his sons at his deathbed (cf. Gen. 49) . The blessing was mentioned, and the Nuzi court upheld it as legally binding.

Abraham's purchase of a burial plot from Ephron the Hittite has been explained as a result of a study of the Hittite Law Code by Manfred R. Lehman. The code, discovered at the ancient Hittite capital at Boghazkoy dates back to the fourteenth century B.C., but the laws it embodies are evidently much older. The law states that certain feudal services must be performed by the owner of a piece of real estate. If the land is transferred, the new owner must assume the feudal obligation. If, however, the new owner purchases only a portion of the property, feudal obligations continue for the former owner. Abraham specified that he wished to purchase only the cave at the edge of Ephron's field (Gen. 23:9) . Ephron insisted, however, "I sell you the field, and I sell you the cave which is in it" (Gen. 23:11) . He evidently saw the possibility of ridding himself of feudal obligations, and insisted that Abraham purchase the entire field, or none of it. Hittite business documents list the exact number of trees in each real estate transaction. The mention of the trees (Gen. 23:17) in connection with Abraham's purchase of Ephron's field conforms with this custom.

In making payment for the field we read that Abraham weighed out the price (coinage of money had not been invented) , with the added note that the silver was "current money with the merchant" (Gen. 23:16) . During the Patriarchal Age commercial men traveled extensively throughout the Fertile Crescent and in Asia Minor. Silver as a medium of exchange had to meet certain specifications to be "standard" for such business transactions.

With the spiritual concept of a covenant with God which included not only the individual but his "seed" or posterity, marriage was a solemn institution in the eyes of the Biblical patriarchs. The father would assume the responsibility for arranging a suitable marriage for his son. Particular care was taken that marriage with the idolatrous inhabitants of Canaan be avoided. Thus Abraham sent his servant to distant Paddan-aram to find a suitable bride for Isaac (Gen. 24) . There were, of course, sons who did not submit to parental discipline in this respect. Esau grieved his father and mother by marrying, obviously without their consent, two native Hittite girls (Gen. 26:34) . His brother Jacob, on the other hand, personally went to the Paddan-aram area where he chose his own bride – the lovely Rachel – although the crafty Laban tricked him into taking her less attractive sister first.

The father of a prospective bride was given a *mohar* (usually fifty shekels) which served as compensation for the loss of his daughter. This *mohar* was not necessarily paid in silver, for Jacob was able to exchange fourteen years of labor for Leah and Rachel (Gen. 29:20, 27, 30). Although the *mohar* was not, strictly speaking, regarded as a "bride price" in Israel, the custom evidently goes back to a time when brides were purchased. The law code of Eshnunna specified that a prospective groom pay "bride money" with the stipulation that it be returned to him with 20 percent interest in the event that the bride died.

Frequently the father of the bride bestowed gifts upon his daughter which would, practically speaking, result in a return of part of the *mohar*. Rebekah, Leah, and Rachel all brought female slaves with them when they left their father's home (Gen. 24:61; 29:23, 29).

The purpose of marriage in the ancient Near East was not to provide companionship, but rather to insure the survival of the family by the provision of male descendants. This is evident both in the Nuzi marriage contracts with their stipulation that a childless wife must provide an handmaid for her husband, and in the concept of levirate marriage where the next of kin must father a child for the man who died without issue.

The wife was an important member of the family, both as mother and worker. The romantic account of the choice of a bride for Isaac actually hinges on the willingness of the young lady to work hard. The sign which Abraham's servant posited as the means by which he would recognize the young lady of God's choice was simple and direct:

> Behold, I am standing by the spring of water, and the daughters of the men of the city are coming out to draw water. Let the maiden to whom I shall say, "Pray let down your jar that I may drink," and who shall say, "Drink, and I will water your camels" — let her be the one whom thou hast appointed for thy servant Isaac (Gen. 24:14).

Camels, of course, travel long without water, and when they are watered they drink large amounts. Rebekah took an exceptionally hard manual chore upon herself when she offered to bring water for the camels. This was interpreted as the sign that she was the girl for Isaac.

The settlement of the *mohar* payment was a decisive element in betrothal. Abraham's servant provided costly gifts for Rebekah's brother and her mother (Gen. 24:53) as well as the young lady herself. They all enjoyed a banquet (Gen. 24:54) after which the young lady herself was asked if she would go to Canaan to become the wife of Isaac (Gen. 24:57). This may not have been legally necessary but considerate parents then, as now, would not ride roughshod over the desires of their children in so important a matter.

Betrothal in antiquity was a more serious arrangement than the modern concept of engagement. A woman who was found to be unfaithful after betrothal was punished as an adulteress (Deut. 22:23-27). If the bridegroom died before marriage could be consummated, the girl was regarded as a member of his family and had the rights and obligations imposed by the concept of levirate marriage.

Levirate marriage was designed to perpetuate the name of the deceased husband in Israel, and to keep his property intact so that it could be passed on to the next generation. When a man died without having fathered children, it was the obligation of his brother or next of kin to marry the widow. The first son of the second marriage was reckoned by law to the first husband, whose name he bore and whose property he inherited.

A vivid illustration of levirate marriage is presented in Genesis 38. Judah obtained a girl named Tamar to be the wife of his firstborn son, Er. When Er died without progeny, Tamar was married to her husband's younger brother, Onan. He, too, died childless, and Tamar was sent to her father's house to wait until Judah's third son, Shelah, reached maturity.

Judah, however, seems to have hesitated to arrange for the marriage of Shelah to Tamar. Perhaps he felt that she was in some way responsible for the death of her first two husbands. When Tamar suspected that Shelah was being withheld from her, she determined to take things in her own hands. She disguised herself as a prostitute, seduced her father-in-law, Judah, and in due time bore twin sons.

When Judah learned that his daughter-in-law was pregnant, he was indignant at her evident infidelity. Confronted with the evidence of what had actually happened, he had to admit, "She is more in the right than I" (Gen. 38:26). While not condoning the means she used in getting a son, he recognized that he had been in the wrong in keeping Shelah from Tamar. We actually learn from the Hittite code that when there was no brother-in-law to perform the levirate duty, the father-in-law was responsible to do so.

Nuzi marriage contracts sometimes specify that the woman purchased by a man for his son shall, if widowed, pass on to a second and, if necessary, a third son. The custom also appears in the Middle Assyrian and the Hittite law codes as well as in the Mosaic law (Deut. 25:5-10). It doubtless goes back to a period when a woman who was purchased in marriage belonged permanently to the family of the man who bought her.

We do not read of any wedding ceremony at the time of the patriarchs. The veiled bride was brought into the tent of her groom and they were regarded as man and wife (Gen. 24:22, 65). At a later time we read that Samson propounded a riddle to be solved within the "seven days of the feast" (Judg. 14:12) which served as a part of the marriage celebration. When responding to Jacob's protest that he had labored for Rachel and had received Leah instead, Laban replied, "Complete the week of this one, and we will give you the other also in return for serving me another seven years" (Gen. 29:27). Evidently Laban wished Jacob to go through with the week of festivities arranged for Leah's wedding, with the assurance that the matter of Jacob's desire for Rachel could then be given due attention. Marriage in patriarchal times, as now, should be a joyful time in which the blessings of God receive due recognition.

12

THE GOD WHOM THE PATRIARCHS WORSHIPED

The religious concepts of the patriarchs contain the germ of later Israelite and Christian faith. Their attitudes were unsophisticated, and the institutionalized elements of a religion with an established priesthood and a central sanctuary were in the distant future. The Bible teaches us that the ancestors of the patriarchs were idolators (Josh. 24:2, 14). Names such as Terah and Laban (both derived from words for the moon) suggest that the moon god was worshiped at one time. The fact that the Sumerian moon god, Nanna, was the patron deity of both Ur and Haran is consistent with this suggestion.

A variety of names for the God worshiped by the patriarchs appears in the book of Genesis. Sometimes the deity is specifically related to his worshiper. On the basis of this fact, Albrecht Alt has suggested that each of the patriarchs had a separate cult in which the deity had a name compounded with the personal name of his worshiper: The Shield of Abraham (Gen. 15:1); the Fear *(paḥad)* of Isaac (Gen. 31:42, 53; Albright translates "Kinsman of Isaac"); and the Champion (or Strong One) of Jacob (Gen. 49:24). According to Alt these deities were originally regarded as separate entities but they were subsequently fused into the concept of Yahweh, the God of Israel.

Although this scheme is widely followed today, it actually says little about the ancestral faith of the Israelites. The Biblical text itself contains no hint that each Israelite regarded his own deity as one god among many. There are, on the contrary, amazing instances in which the gods of others are identified with the God they worshiped.

After rescuing Lot from a confederation of eastern kings who had conquered and despoiled Sodom, Abraham paid a visit to Salem where he paid tithes to the priest-king of the city, Melchizedek. Although there is no hint that the two had ever met before, Abraham recognized Melchizedek as a true priest. Yet Melchizedek was a priest of El Elyon ("God most high") who, he declared, had given Abraham victory over his enemies (Gen. 14:20). Later, Abraham reported that he had made a vow to Yahweh-El Elyon (Gen. 14:22; R.S.V. renders the name "The Lord God Most High"). This is a clear instance of a fusion of two divine names which Abraham appears to have done consciously because he could identify the two names as representative of one deity. The patriarch could recognize the validity of Melchizedek's ministry even though he used a different name for God from that usually employed by Abraham.

It is quite possible that Abraham shared many of the erroneous views concerning religious matters which characterized the age in which he lived. The fact that he received a revelation from God did not render him omniscient. It was the faith of Abraham, however, augmented by subsequent revelation, which became the basis for all subsequent Jewish, Christian, and even Moslem thought.

The differences between the faith of Abraham, and that of the Canaanites among whom he lived, can hardly be exaggerated, however. Their religion was based on the cult of Baal, a fertility god, and had, as a practical purpose, the insuring of the fertility of the fields, man, and beast. Abraham's faith had a historical basis. God had entered history and issued a call which Abraham was bound to obey.

The relationship between Abraham and the God he worshiped was based on the concept of covenant. It is known that covenant formed an important element in the social and political life of the ancient Near East. In nomadic societies we often find clans regularizing their relations with one another by means of a covenant (cf. Gen. 31:44-54).

George Mendenhall of the University of Michigan has made a study of covenants in the ancient Near East during the second millennium B.C. They are found to fall into two categories: the parity treaty (between equals), and the suzerainty treaty (between a king and his vassals). The treaty between Jacob and Laban, in which each agreed to honor a stated frontier, would be classed as a parity treaty. The covenant between Yahweh and Israel, however, would be a suzerainty treaty. God is recognized as the gracious yet all-powerful King of his people, and they are expected to obey his command.

Genesis 15 contains the record of a ceremony by which God and Abraham entered into solemn covenant relationships. Abraham was instructed to cut in two a number of animals and place the halves opposite one another. After the sun had set, the divine Presence in the form of "a smoking fire pot and a flaming torch" passed between the pieces (Gen. 15:17). In this way God was depicted in the act of ratifying the covenant. The terms of the covenant were actually very simple. God identified himself as the One who had brought Abraham from Ur of the Chaldees to give to him the land of Canaan, and Abraham was promised a progeny comparable in number to the stars in heaven.

The covenant between God and Abraham would be, in Mendenhall's terminology, a suzerainty treaty. It finds its origin in the will of the suzerain (God) who recounts his gracious acts (taking Abraham from Ur) and declares his purposes with reference to Abraham. The patriarch is expected to exercise faith in the divine promise.

Mendenhall's studies have particular reference, however, to the Mosaic Law, which is presented in terms which frequently form an exact parallel to ancient suzerainty treaties. Some scholars, considering the Mosaic formulation the first such covenant in Israelite history, have argued that the Biblical references to covenants in the Patriarchal Age are a retrojection of concepts which were held at a later time. There are important differences between the two, however. The patriarchal covenants are personal in nature, and largely future in fulfillment, demanding only the trust of the worshiper. The Sinai covenant was based on a past act of redemption (the Exodus from Egypt) and embodied a full legal formulation. It was addressed to the entire Israelite people.

Covenant solidarity between God and his people is illustrated by the names used by the Israelites and their northwest Semitic neighbors. Many such names begin with Ab (father), Aḥ (brother) and Amm (people, or family). A name such as Eliezer ("my God is a help") may be compared with Abiezer ("my [divine] Father is a help"). An Israelite prophet actually bore the name Ahijah ("my brother is Yahweh"). A generation which stresses the transcendence of God may find such names unduly familiar, but they do illustrate the conception of kinship between a man and his deity which was characteristic of the patriarchal faith.

13

THE PATRIARCHAL INSTITUTIONS

Formal aspects of patriarchal religion were surprisingly few. The patriarchs are presented to us as men of prayer, and they habitually build altars on which sacrifices are made to God. No details are given concerning the nature of the sacrifices, however, and the head of the family uniformly acted as his own priest. Job, whose life has much in common with the patriarchs, is dipicted as arising early in the morning and offering burnt offerings for his children (Job 1:5).

1. Prayer

Prayer is expressive of an attitude of dependence upon the Lord. The fact that, in the days of Seth, "men began to call upon the name of the Lord" (Gen. 4:26), implies that there have been times and places where prayer and worship have been neglected. Prayer is, in its very essence, fellowship with God. When sin mars that fellowship we find man hiding from his Creator (Gen. 3:10). The absence of prayer marks a secular individual or society.

During the age of the Biblical patriarchs, prayer formed a most important part of life. Although frequently associated with sacrifice (Gen. 12:8; 13:4), prayer was not a formalized rite but rather a free, spontaneous communication between man and his God. It was a dialogue in which we meet argumentation as well as conversation.

Not only was there no set form of words, but the prayers of the patriarchs could be offered from a variety of postures. When Abraham received word of the impending judgment on Sodom he "stood before the Lord" (Gen. 18:22) and talked with Him as a man might talk to his associate. The servant who had been sent to Paddan-aram to find a suitable wife for Isaac, when conscious that God had prospered his journey, "bowed his head and worshiped the Lord" (Gen. 24:26). He showed a spirit of humble thankfulness to the God who had met his need and that of his master.

Sometimes we are surprised at the fact that the patriarchs actually argue or talk back to God. When God addressed Abraham with the words, "Fear not . . . your reward shall be very great," the patriarch replied, "O Lord God, what wilt thou give me, for I continue childless . . ." (Gen. 15:1-2). The promises of God seemed idle to Abraham because he had no heir, and the patriarch did not hesitate to make the fact known to God. Thereupon, we read, the Lord brought Abraham out into the oriental night and said, "Look toward heaven, and number the stars, if you are able to number them. So shall your descendants be," was the assurance which Abraham accepted by faith. God, we are told, "reckoned it to him for righteousness" (Gen. 15:5-6).

Much of the prayer mentioned in the patriarchal records is in the form of intercession. When God told Abraham that Sarah, his wife, would give birth to a son, the patriarch's response was a supplication, "Oh that Ishmael might live before thee" (Gen. 17:18). God made it clear that Ishmael would be blessed in his own way (Gen. 17:20-21), but that the covenant blessing would continue through the line of Isaac (Gen. 17:19).

The declaration that Sodom was to be destroyed, brought a petition from Abraham that it be spared if fifty righteous men could be found in the city (Gen. 18:24-25). Abraham argued that God must do "right" since He is the Judge of all the earth, implying that it would not be "right" for the righteous to perish with the wicked. God replied that the city would be spared if as few as ten righteous men could be found in Sodom (Gen. 18:32). Although ten could not be found, the one righteous family, that of Lot, was removed from the city before destruction came (Gen. 19:15-29). The subsequent tragedies in Lot's experience do not alter the lesson of God's righteousness shown in the deliverance of the family of Lot before the destruction of Sodom.

When Abimelech of Gerar learned that Sarah, whom he had taken for himself, was actually Abraham's wife, he was understandably disturbed. God's comforting word to Abimelech included an assurance of the efficacy of prayer: "Restore the man's wife; for he is a prophet, and he will pray for you, and you shall live" (Gen. 20:7). Abraham is known as the "friend of God" (cf. II Chron. 20:7) and his intercession could be counted on to bring a blessing to Abimelech and his household.

Prayer in the patriarchal records frequently expresses dependence upon God for daily mercies. On his journey to Paddan-aram, Abraham's servant prayed, "O Lord, God of my master Abraham, grant me success today" (Gen. 24:12). Abraham had sent him to find a suitable bride for Isaac, and the servant sought divine wisdom on so important an undertaking. Later, when arrangements were being made to take Rebekah back to Canaan, he testified, "The Lord has prospered my way" (Gen. 24:56).

Vows and prayers were often closely related. At Bethel, Jacob, fleeing from the brother he had wronged, saw a vision of a ladder which reached from earth to heaven, and heard the voice of the Lord saying, "I am the Lord, the God of Abraham your father and the God of Isaac; the land on which you lie will I give to you and to your descendants" (Gen. 28:11-13). The Lord further promised to be with Jacob during his journeys and to bring him back safely to the land of Canaan. Humbled, yet encouraged at this awesome experience, Jacob arose the next morning and vowed, "If God will be with me, and will keep me in this way that I go, and will give me bread to eat and clothing to wear, so that I come again to my father's house in peace, then the Lord shall be my God" (Gen. 28:20-22).

Sometimes fear is a factor in prayer. The consciousness of a lack of ability to cope with the circumstances of life may cause us to seek the face of God in prayer. During the years which Jacob spent in Paddan-aram, Esau, whom he had defrauded, was a hazy memory. As Jacob moved toward Canaan again, the possibility of an encounter with his brother became a fearful prospect. In anguish he prayed, "O God of my father Abraham, and God of my father Isaac, O Lord who didst say to me, 'Return to your country and to your kindred, and I will do you good,' I am not worthy of the least of all the steadfast love and all the faithfulness which thou hast shown to thy servant, for with only my staff I have crossed this Jordan; and now I have become two companies. Deliver me, I pray thee, from the hand of my brother, from the hand of Esau. . . ." (Gen. 32:9-12).

This prayer was in part answered during a strange nocturnal experience on the shore of the Jabbok when Jacob, alone, wrestled with a "man" (Gen. 32:24). During the encounter Jacob sought, and received, a blessing and a new name (Israel) from the stranger whom he identified with God Himself (Gen. 32:30).

2. Sacrifice

The concept of sacrifice, regularized by the Mosaic law, appears on the earliest pages of Scripture. Cain and Abel each offered a *minḥah* ("offering") to the Lord, although only that of Abel was accepted (Gen. 4:3-5). This serves as a reminder that the presentation of a sacrifice was never accounted meritorious in itself. The spirit of the worshiper was most important. Isaiah as the spokesman of God cried out to his generation, "I have had enough of burnt offerings of rams and the fat of fed beasts; I do not delight in the blood of bulls, or of lambs, or of he-goats.... Bring no more vain oblations" (Isa. 1:11-13).

The abuse of sacrifice, however, did not mean that its use was not encouraged under the Old Testament economy. Man, in his sacrifice, presented a portion of his own property to the God who is the author of every perfect gift. In the choice of the sacrifice man chose a gift which he deemed fit to present to God. Under the Levitical laws (Lev. 1:1-7:37) the appropriate sacrifices for various occasions and individuals were prescribed.

Following the flood we read that Noah offered *'oloth,* "burnt offerings" to the Lord. As its name implies, the burnt offering was slain and then totally burned on an altar. The worshiper thus gave a portion of his property and, in a sense, of himself to God. The very death of the victim may be a reminder, as it certainly was on the Day of Atonement (Lev. 16:1-22), that the worshiper is worthy of death, and that God is pleased to accept the life of the slain beast as a substitute for the sinner who has broken the divine law.

Sacrifice was a regular part of the worship of Abraham and the Israelite patriarchs. After the theophany at Shechem, in which God said, "Unto thy seed will I give this land," we read that Abraham "built there an altar unto the Lord" (Gen. 12:7). Later altars were built at Bethel (Gen. 12:8; 13:18).

After his unpleasant experiences with Abimelech of Gerar, Isaac settled at Beer-sheba where again we read of a theophany. God identified himself as "the God of Abraham," and assured Isaac of divine protection and the fact that his "seed" would be multiplied (Gen. 26:24). As his father Abraham had done, Isaac "built an altar there and called upon the name of the Lord" (Gen. 26:25).

Laban was angered at the departure of Jacob from Paddan-aram. He pursued the patriarch as far as to Mizpah where a satisfactory settlement was reached. Laban accepted the fact that Jacob, with his wives, children, and possessions, was returning home to Canaan, and suggested that the two men make a covenant of peace. In concluding the terms of their covenant, "Jacob offered a sacrifice on the mountain and called his kinsmen to eat bread; and they ate bread and tarried all night on the mountain" (Gen. 31:54).

After the sad experience at Shechem, where Simeon and Levi killed the Shechemites because of the defilement of Dinah, their sister, Jacob heard the voice of God saying, "Arise, go up to Bethel, and dwell there and make there an altar to the God who appeared to you when you fled from your brother Esau" (Gen. 35:1). Subsequently Jacob and his sons moved to Bethel where they built an altar which they named, "El Beth-el" ("God of the House of God"). In this way they commemorated the grace of God in bringing them safely back to Bethel.

We subsequently read of an altar built at Beer-sheba where Jacob "offered sacrifices to the God of his father Isaac" (Gen. 46:1). Here God appeared to the patriarch and directed that he go down with his sons to Egypt where Joseph had become Vizier (Prime Minister).

Adolphe Lods, in his work *Israel from its Beginnings to the Middle of the Eighth Century,* says concerning the pre-Mosaic Israelites, "their religion must already have contained, even if in a somewhat barbarous and elementary form, the greater part of the rites which were later codified in the Levitical law."[1] Although the term "barbarous" would be more applicable to the Canaanites than to Israel, the Scriptures make it clear that faith and Law long antedate Moses and Sinai.

Abraham's journey with Isaac to Mount Moriah marks an important chapter in the concept of sacrifice. To Micah's question, "Shall I give my first-born for my transgression, the fruit of my body for the sin of my soul?" (Micah 6:7), the Scripture answers, "No." As late as the time of Jeremiah, the Judaeans, "built the high places of Baal to burn their sons in the fire" (Jer. 19:5). This had been prohibited by the Law (cf. Lev. 20:1-5). When Abraham had taken Isaac to Mount Moriah, ready to offer his own son on a stone altar, God said, "Do not lay your hand on the lad" (Gen. 22:12), and a ram caught in a nearby thicket served as a substitute. Although individuals under pagan influence frequently lapsed into heathen practices, the prophets of Israel consistently denounced human sacrifice.

1. Adolphe Lods, *Israel from its Beginnings to the Middle of the Eighth Century,* p. 277.

Just as there are certain points which the moral law of the Old Testament has in common with contemporary law codes of the Fertile Crescent lands, so we find certain ceremonial laws in use at ancient Ugarit which have a resemblance to those of the Mosaic Law. The Ugaritic documents (15th and 14th centuries B.C.) speak of a Burnt Offering, a Whole Burnt Offering, a Guilt Offering, and a Peace Offering.

It should be remembered, however, that the Mosaic law did not originate the concept of sacrifice in Israel. As in the instance of the moral law, much of the ceremonial law recorded in Exodus and Leviticus is actually a codification of practices which had been observed from much earlier times. Sacrifice was in use at the earliest levels of Biblical history and was a normal occurrence during the Patriarchal Age.

3. Circumcision

The rite of circumcision became the sign of the covenant between the Lord and Abraham. Physically it involved the removal of the foreskin of the male organ of reproduction. Spiritually it became the sign which designated the individual who had associated himself with the people of Israel.

The rite of circumcision was practiced by many peoples of antiquity, usually at the time of puberty. The fact that it was often regarded as a preparation for marriage may be inferred from the fact that the Semitic word for bridegroom *(ḥathen)* literally means "circumcised," and the corresponding word for father-in-law *(ḥothen)* literally means "he who circumcises." Among the neighbors of Israel who practiced circumcision in ancient times were the Edomites, Ammonites, Moabites, and Egyptians. The "uncircumcised Philistine" was, of course, an exception.

Among the Israelites, circumcision was practiced on the eighth day of a child's life (Gen. 17:12). All male Israelites, including slaves, were circumcised, as were any foreigners who might wish to be associated with Israel in the observance of the Passover (Exod. 12:48). Thus circumcision became the external mark of citizenship in Israel.

Circumcision marked Israel as the covenant people of the Old Testament economy. It was established as a covenant sign to Abraham who was to become, according to divine promise, "a great nation" and through whom, it was stated, "all the families of the earth will bless themselves" (Gen. 12:2-3). The practice of the rite from generation to generation served as a continuing reminder of the promises of God and of his constant faithfulness.

Circumcision, like sacrifices, could be rendered meaningless if it was reduced to a mere ritual. Jeremiah complained of his generation that "all the house of Israel is uncircumcised in heart" (Jer. 9:26). Similarly the book of Deuteronomy, after recounting the fearful consequences of disobedience to the Law of the Lord, speaks of a day when Israel will be restored: "And the Lord your God will circumcise your heart and the heart of your offspring, so that you will love the Lord your God with all your heart and with all your soul, that you may live" (Deut. 30:6).

14

THE THEOLOGY OF THE PATRIARCHS

The Bible student who reads the patriarchal records (Gen. 12-50) is aware of the fact that the men whose lives it records were not given to philosophical speculation. There is no hint of a "systematic theology" in the sense in which that term is now used. The concern of the patriarchs was with a God who had revealed himself to them, and with their response to that revelation. God was not a remote "first cause" to be believed or rejected, but a Person who was as real as any member of the family.

Although God was in a very personal sense "the God of Abraham," the patriarch saw in Him a God whose interests far exceeded any tribal limitations. He was "maker of heaven and earth" (Gen. 14:19) and he purposed to bring blessing to "all the families of the earth" (Gen. 12:3). Abraham thought in terms of the laws of nature when he questioned the possibility of having a son because of his own advanced age and that of Sarah, his wife. When Sarah incredulously exclaimed, "Shall I indeed bear a child now that I am old?" (Gen. 18:13), God replied with a question, "Is anything too hard for the Lord?" (Gen. 18:14).

God's omnipotence was also evident during Abraham's sojourn in Egypt. The patriarch had lied concerning the true identity of Sarah with the thought that he might save his own life by so doing (Gen. 12:10-16). When Pharaoh took Sarah, purposing to add her to his harem, "the Lord afflicted Pharaoh and his house with great plagues" (Gen. 12:17). The patriarchs learned that God was omnipotent, and that his purposes were sure because there was no limit to his power.

The omniscience of God is also constantly before us in the patriarchal records. He knows the future, and can tell in advance of the birth of Isaac to Sarah (Gen. 17:19). Although, in the language of anthropomorphism, God is pictured as coming down to investigate the sins of Sodom and Gomorrah (Gen. 18:21), it is clear that He does this because of His knowledge that "their sin is very grave" (Gen. 18:20). The "investigation" does not reflect upon his knowledge, but rather emphasizes his justice. As a human judge must secure all the facts before passing sentence, so the "Judge of all the earth" will surely "do right" (Gen. 18:25).

The judgment on the city of Sodom reflects the holiness and justice of God. This was not an act of impatience, or a severe punishment for a minor offense. The record states that "the outcry against Sodom and Gomorrah is great, and their sin is very grave" (Gen. 18:20). When Lot provided hospitality for the two "angels" who came to Sodom, we read that "the men of the city . . . both young and old, all the people to the last man, surrounded the house" (Gen. 19:4) and sought carnal relations with them.

The justice of God is tempered, however, with mercy. Had there been ten righteous men in Sodom, the city would have been spared (Gen. 18:32). God appeared to the fugitive Jacob at Bethel with the assurance, "Behold, I am with you and will keep you wherever you go, and will bring you back to this land" (Gen. 28:15). When he was about to offer his son as a sacrifice, Abraham heard the voice of God saying, "Do not lay your hand on the lad or do anything to him" (Gen. 22:12). The ram in the thicket became the offering, and Isaac was set free.

When Abraham's servant met Rebekah by a well in distant Paddan-aram, he testified saying, "The Lord has led me in the way to the house of my master's kinsmen" (Gen. 24:27). The patriarchs were conscious of a God who directed their every step. This did not result in a neglect of attention to secondary causes. It is clear that Jacob had to flee from Canaan because of the wrath of Esau, whom he had defrauded of the birthright (Gen. 27:41-45). Yet Jacob was assured of the continuing presence of God in his journeys (Gen. 28:15).

Cause and effect are clearly seen in the story of Joseph. The fact that Joseph was the favored son quite understandably made his brethren jealous. The jealousy reached a climax when they determined to murder him and then, through the counsel of Judah, sold him into slavery instead. From the human point of view, Joseph went to Egypt because of the jealousy of his brothers and their sinful determination to get rid of him.

Parallel to the story of the sinful purposes of the brethren is the story of the gracious purposes of God: "The Lord was with Joseph, and he became a successful man" (Gen. 39:2). God's providence was frequently hidden, however. After arising to a place of trust in Potiphar's household, Joseph was the object of false witness, accused of immorality, and consigned to prison. Even this, however, is interpreted as a part of the sovereign purposes of God, and we still read, "the Lord was with him, and whatever he did, the Lord made it to prosper" (Gen. 39:23).

When called upon to interpret Pharaoh's dream, Joseph provided the counsel which made it possible for Egypt to have food during a time of famine. Other peoples, including Joseph's own brethren, looked to Egypt for deliverance from starvation. In making himself known to his brethren, Joseph said, ". . . do not be distressed or angry with yourselves, because you sold me here; for God sent me before you to preserve life. . . . So it was not you who sent me here, but God. . . ." (Gen. 45:4-8). Joseph was able to look behind the sinful intent of his brothers and see his presence in Egypt as part of the purpose of an all-powerful, all-gracious God.

Although the patriarchal period antedates the Mosaic Law, there is no lack of concern about the heinousness of sin. The destruction of Sodom (Gen. 19) illustrated God's attitude toward sin.

An important principle concerning sin is expressed at the time of the ratification of God's covenant with Abraham (Gen. 15:7-21). The descendants of Abraham would one day possess the land of Canaan, but the patriarch, himself, would not live to see that time. The reason for the delay in giving the land to Abraham is stated in the words, ". . . the iniquity of the Amorites is not yet complete" (Gen. 15:16). The statement is prophetic, implying that one day (and, in the context, specifically, in "the fourth generation"), the sins of the inhabitants of Canaan will be such that God will drive them out and give their land to Israel. The further principle that expulsion would result only when the sin proved incorrigible illustrates the long-suffering of God with sinful mankind.

Man, in the patriarchal records, is a creature wholly dependent on and subject to God. The command to Abraham was, "Walk before me and be blameless" (Gen. 17:1). This meant that the patriarch had to leave home and loved ones, and wander in a foreign country (Gen. 12:1). Abraham had to dismiss the beloved Ishmael (Gen. 17:18; 20:10-14), and, subsequently, he was directed to offer Isaac as a sacrifice on Mount Moriah (Gen. 22:1-14).

The promises to the patriarchs were largely of a material nature. God promised to Abraham countless descendants (Gen. 15:5) who would have great possessions (Gen. 15:14), including the entire land of Canaan (Gen. 13:14-17). This is called "the land of promise" (Heb. 11:9), because Abraham did not personally live to see his descendants possess it. Abraham was but a sojourner, looking with the eye of faith to the time when God's purposes would be fulfilled.

Little is said concerning the attitude of the patriarchs to life beyond the grave. Of Abraham we read that he "died in a good old age, an old man and full of years, and was gathered to his people" (Gen. 25:7). When Jacob received evidence that convinced him of the death of Joseph, he said, "... I shall go down to Sheol, to my son, mourning" (Gen. 37:35). Not until the death and resurrection of Christ do we find the full-orbed doctrine of resurrection which elicited the confident outcry of Paul, "To me to live is Christ, and to die is gain" (Phil. 1:21).

The faith of the patriarchs was oriented toward the future. Although promised the entire land of Palestine, Abraham owned no real estate except the parcel of ground which he purchased from Ephron the Hittite (Gen. 23:3-16).

Promises concerning the future were related to the idea of a "seed" or descendants through whom blessing would flow to all families of the earth (Gen. 12:1-3). There is, indeed, within the patriarchal records both a particularistic and a universalistic strain. The particularistic was immediate – the line of the faithful must not intermarry with the wicked Canaanites (Gen. 24:1-4). The grounds were religious, however, and not racial. If Israel felt an obligation to maintain separation from her neighbors it was, ideally at least, because she was conscious of a God-given mission which required absolute separation from idolatry and all forms of heathen religious life. During the later Exodus period this was made explicit: "You shall not do as they do in the land of Egypt, where you dwelt, and you shall not do as they do in the land of Canaan, to which I am bringing you" (Lev. 18:3). Pre-exilic Israel tended to forget this injunction, until things became so bad that Jeremiah cried out, "... as many as your cities are your gods, O Judah" (Jer. 2:28).

The universalistic strain of patriarchal faith is an advance beyond anything we know in the ancient world. We not only meet the general statements of blessings to the families of the earth, but we read specifically of blessings upon non-Israelite peoples. When God made it clear that Isaac, not Ishmael, would be the child of the covenant line, a blessing was also pronounced upon Ishmael: "I will bless him and make him fruitful and multiply him exceedingly; he shall be the father of twelve princes, and I will make him a great nation" (Gen. 17:20).

The blessing which Isaac meant for Esau fell, by trickery, on Jacob, with the result that little was left for Esau. Yet even here we read a kind of negative blessing: "By your sword you shall live, and you shall serve your brother; but when you break loose you shall break his yoke from your neck" (Gen. 27:40). Esau would be subject to Jacob, or, translated into later political history, Edom would be subject to Israel (later to Judah, the southern kingdom), but the Edomites would regain their freedom. The prophet Obadiah describes the way in which proud, independent Edom stood aloof while the Babylonians plundered Judah and Jerusalem.

The covenant line of the patriarchs – Abraham, Isaac, and Jacob – was distinct, but Ishmael and Esau became great peoples. From Jacob our covenant line breaks into twelve parts, one of which (Levi) becomes the priestly tribe and another (Judah) becomes the tribe of King David. Each of the tribes is considered a part of Israel, however, and the covenant made at Mount Sinai embodies all.

It is beyond even these, however, that the blessings of Abraham ultimately reach. The patriarchs did not fill in the details concerning the nature of their hope. Their descendants would go to Egypt (Gen. 15:13), but they would return and, in some future day, the "seed" of Abraham would bring blessing which would transcend all tribal boundaries and reach to all mankind.

It was this patriarchal blessing which was in the mind of the New Testament writers who stressed the relationship of Jesus to Abraham. In Matthew's genealogy, Jesus is linked with David, the king, and with Abraham, to whom the promise of blessing was first given (Matt. 1:1). Jesus is thus presented as the Messianic king and the promised "seed of Abraham."

The apostle Paul insists that "in Christ Jesus the blessing of Abraham [has] come upon the gentiles" (Gal. 3:14). He looks upon the promise of blessing through Abraham's "seed" as finding its ultimate fulfillment not simply in the large number of descendants of Abraham, but in the one "seed" of Abraham – Jesus Christ – through whom blessings were mediated to "all families of the earth." Indeed the non-Jew may actually, by faith, be blessed with Abraham, the man of faith (Gal. 3:9). In this latter sense it is the spiritual relationship of the individual to

Abraham that is meaningful, and all "families of the earth" may actually account themselves one with Abraham on the basis of faith in the promises of God.

15

THE PATRIARCHS AND DIVINE REVELATION

The Epistle to the Hebrews begins with the assertion that it was "at sundry times and in divers manners" that God spoke to the fathers (Heb. 1:1). The writer was stressing the fact that Jesus is God's final revelation, and that the revelations of the Old Testament economy were, of necessity, incomplete. He affirms, however, that the partial revelations through the prophets were, indeed, the Word of God.

The patriarchal records consistently presuppose a God who speaks to his children. Stephen, testifying before a Jewish High Priest, said, ". . . the God of glory appeared to our father Abraham, when he was in Mesopotamia, before he lived in Haran, and said to him, Depart from your land and from your kindred and go into the land which I will show you" (Acts 7:2).

Often the patriarchal narrative mentions the fact of revelation, with no clue as to the means by which it is accomplished. When we read that, "the Lord said to Abram, go from your country and your kindred, and your father's house" (Gen. 12:1), we are not told whether God spoke in a dream, a vision, an audible voice, or a theophany. The fact, rather than the means, of revelation is stressed.

Subsequently, however, we read that the Lord "appeared" to Abraham (Gen. 12:7). Such appearances were sometimes associated with visible manifestations. In ratifying the covenant with Abraham, we read, "behold, a smoking fire pot and a flaming torch passed between these pieces" (Gen. 15:17). God, in the form of fire, consumed the sacrifice which Abraham had offered to seal the covenant.

The close relationship between Abraham and his God is reflected in the description of the patriarch as "the friend of God" (James 2:23). The Arabs have named him *El-Khalil* ("the friend").

The term theophany is frequently used in describing visible appearances of God to man. In Genesis 17:1 we read that the Lord "appeared" to Abram, changed his name to Abraham, promised the land of Canaan as an inheritance to his descendants, and established circumcision as the sign of the covenant. He further declared that Sarai, whose name was changed to Sarah, would bear a son who would become Abraham's heir. The account of the theophany closes with the words, "When he had finished talking with him, God went up from Abraham" (Gen. 17:22). The episode presupposes that Abraham and his God speak face to face.

The appearance of three "men" at the door of Abraham's tent (Gen. 18:2), caused the patriarch to make elaborate preparation for their entertainment. He was not aware, of course, that the Lord was appearing in this way (Gen. 18:1). One of these "men" prophesied that Sarah would give birth to a son (Gen. 18:10). Before leaving, the Lord (evidently to be identified as one of the "men"), told Abraham of impending judgment upon Sodom (Gen. 18:17). Thereupon Abraham interceded on behalf of the wicked city, praying that it might be spared if as few as ten righteous men might be found there (Gen. 18:22-32). Then we read, "And the Lord went his way when he had finished speaking to Abraham, and Abraham returned to his place (Gen. 18:33).

We read of subsequent appearances of God to Isaac, warning him not to go to Egypt (Gen. 26:2) and assuring him of protection and blessing (Gen. 26:34). When Jacob was sleeping at Bethel, he dreamed of a ladder which reached from earth to heaven. Above the ladder he saw a theophany. The One who spoke identified himself as the God of Abraham and Isaac, and assured Jacob that the land of Canaan would become the inheritance of his descendants (Gen. 28:13). Many years later, Jacob testified, "God almighty appeared to me at Luz in the land of Canaan, and blessed me" (Gen. 48:3).

The term "angel of the Lord" is frequently used to describe the characteristic form of theophany during the patriarchal period. When Hagar was fleeing from Sarah she met the Angel of the Lord, who commanded her to return to her mistress. The angel told Hagar she would give birth to a son, Ishmael, who would be a strong, outdoor man (the term "wild ass of a man" is not an insult). Hagar identified the Angel with God himself, and returned as she had been commanded (Gen. 16:1-14).

After Abraham had shown his willingness to offer Isaac on Mount Moriah, we read that "the angel of the Lord called to him from heaven" (Gen. 22:11), commanding him to spare the lad. Abraham offered a ram which had been found caught in a nearby thicket, and Isaac was set free. Then, we read, "the angel of the Lord called to Abraham a second time from heaven" (Gen. 22:15) assuring him that his descendants would be a means of blessing to "all the nations of the earth."

Jacob's years at Paddan-aram are not marked by any communication with God but, at the close of that period, when concerned about problems rising from the jealousy of Laban's sons, we read that the "angel of the Lord" spoke to him in a dream, identifying Himself as the God of Bethel, and commanding Jacob to return to the land of his birth (Gen. 31:11-13). In old age, looking back over the joys and heartaches of life, Jacob spoke of "the God who has led me all my life long to this day, the angel who has redeemed me from all evil" (Gen. 48:15-16).

The term "angel of the Lord" or "angel of God" appears to be used, in some contexts at least, as a synonym for God Himself. Geerhardus Vos in his *Biblical Theology* suggests: "If the Angel sent were Himself partaker of the godhead, then He could refer to God as his sender, and at the same time speak as God, and in both cases there would be reality back of it. Without this much of what we call the Trinity, the transaction could not but have been unreal and illusory."[1] Vos makes it clear that he does not consider the disclosure of the Trinity an Old Testament phenomenon. He sees, however, intimations of the Trinity in the patriarchal revelations through the Angel of the Lord.

G. W. Bromiley suggests another explanation of the term Angel of the Lord and its evident reference to God. Bromiley emphasizes the angel as the vehicle of revelation and suggests that, through the angel God speaks so clearly and fully that He, Himself can be said to speak.[2] This, Bromiley feels, better accounts for the usage of the term "Angel of the Lord" in Luke 2:9 where the angel actually heralds the birth of Jesus.

The messages to the patriarchs mediated by the Angel of the Lord, and those in which God himself appears or speaks, are not essentially different. In each instance the authority behind the communication is clearly God Himself.

---

1. Geerhardus Vos, *Biblical Theology*, pp. 86-87.
2. Geoffrey W. Bromiley, "Angel," *Baker's Dictionary of Theology*, pp. 42-43.

16

LAW IN PATRIARCHAL TIMES

The laws which govern the common life of a people afford insights into the values which they hold dear. A legal system which seeks to protect the helpless from the potential despot is itself evidence of a moral sense in the society which avows it. Conversely, a law code which regards wives and slaves as the property of the head of a household reflects a culture in which even the fiction of personal equality is denied.

Ancient law codes, like their modern counterparts, were not always binding. The code represented the ideal, but all evidence indicates that judges had the right to make independent decisions when confronted with specific problems. There is no hint that rulers were expected to master the legal systems of their predecessors, although a legal tradition existed in the Near East from Sumerian times which found expression in the Babylonian code of Hammurabi. Although Biblical law, which deals with moral principles as well as specific infractions, has a different point of reference (the sovereign will of Yahweh who has entered into covenant with His people), there are enough parallels to show that the history of Israel was not isolated from the culture of her neighbors.

1. Ur-nammu

Ur-nammu was the Sumerian ruler who founded the Third Dynasty of Ur, about 2050 B.C. His code, written three centuries before that of the great Babylonian lawgiver, Hammurabi, has been partially preserved in two fragments of a clay tablet now in the Istanbul Museum of the Ancient Orient. The obscure Sumerian writing on the tablet was deciphered by Samuel Noah Kramer of the University of Pennsylvania. It tells how Ur-nammu was chosen by the moon god, Nanna, to rule Ur as his earthly representative.

The first responsibility of Ur-nammu was to defend the boundaries of Ur against encroachments by neighboring Lagash. Having accomplished this, he turned his attention to reforms which were needed within the city-state of Ur. Ur-nammu determined that his government would be marked by justice. The widow and the orphan were not to be neglected. Honest weights and measures were prescribed for the mercantile class of Ur.

The Ur-Nammu law code is in a poor state of preservation, so that only a small fraction of its contents is known. One law seems to refer to the ordeal by water, later mentioned in the Hammurabi code. A woman accused of immorality is cast into the river, which acts as her judge. If the river receives her (i.e., she drowns), her guilt is considered self-evident. If, on the other hand, she swims to shore, she is deemed innocent.

Three of the laws which can be read with a fair degree of accuracy deal with instances of the mutilation of the body. If a man has cut off another man's foot, he is to pay ten shekels. In the Code of Hammurabi such payments are often prescribed when injury is to one of an inferior social status. There the penalty for injury to someone of the same class corresponds to the pattern, "an eye for an eye, and a tooth for a tooth."

The institution of slavery was firmly rooted in the ancient Near East. The victor on the battlefield would normally enslave the conquered army. Slavery, of course, brings many problems with it, and Ur-nammu had to prescribe legislation to deal with the run-away slave, a problem also dealt with in detail in Hammurabi's Code.

2. Eshnunna

Another ancient law code comes from the city-state of Eshnunna which flourished from the end of the Third Dynasty of Ur to the time of the Babylonian king, Hammurabi. Two tablets containing the Eshnunna code were discovered at Tell Abu Harmal, in the Diyala region east of Baghdad by archaeologists from the Iraq Directorate of Antiquities in 1945. Unlike the Ur-nammu code, these tablets were written in the Akkadian language, the Semitic tongue spoken in ancient Assyria and Babylonia. Although we are not certain concerning the date of the Eshnunna code, it is thought to have been promulgated during the reign of Bilalama, about 2000 B.C. Albrecht Goetze, of Yale University, translated them into English.

The code begins with a brief prologue which tells how Tishpak, the chief god of Eshnunna, bestowed upon some ruler (whose name has not been preserved) "the kingship over Eshnunna." It is Goetze's suggestion that the ruler was probably Bilalama.

Sixty paragraphs of the code have been preserved. They deal with such varied subjects as the price of commodities, the wages of labor, the hire of wagons and boats, assault and battery, marriage, divorce, and adultery.

The behavior of oxen and the responsibility of their owners is discussed in the Eshnunna code, in the Code of Hammurabi, and in the Bible.

The Eshnunna Code states:

> If an ox gores an (other) ox, and causes (its) death, both ox owners shall divide (among themselves) the price of the live ox, and also the equivalent of the dead ox. (53)

An exact parallel occurs in the Mosaic law:

> And if one man's ox hurt another's, that he die; then they shall sell the live ox, and divide the money of it; and the dead ox also they shall divide (Exod. 21:35).

It was the responsibility of the owner of oxen to take steps to prevent this from recurring. The Eshnunna code adds:

> If an ox is known to gore habitually, and the authorities have brought the fact to the knowledge of its owner, but he does not have his ox *dehorned,* it bores a man and causes (his) death, then the owner of the ox shall pay two-thirds of a mina of silver. (54)

3. Lipit-Ishtar

During the expedition of the University of Pennsylvania at Nippur in Iraq (1889-1900) fragments of a Sumerian law code were discovered. It was almost a half century later (1947) when the fragments were seriously studied. Samuel N. Kramer announced the discovery of a new Sumerian code in the *Journal of the American Oriental Society,* and Francis Rue Steele, in cooperation with Dr. Kramer, published the edited text in the *American Journal of Archaeology.*[1]

The four fragments found at Nippur were found to be part of the law code of Lipit-Ishtar, the fifth king of the Sumerian city-state of Isin, who reigned for eleven years beginning about 1868 B.C. The code begins with a prologue of almost one hundred lines, most of which have been poorly preserved. It tells

1. Vol. VII, No. 3, July-Sept. 1948.

how Lipit-Ishtar was chosen by the gods Anu and Enlil as the one to "establish justice in the land" and "bring well-being to the Sumerians and the Akkadians."

The code contains thirty-eight paragraphs dealing with such practical matters as the hire of boats, rental of oxen, inheritance, marriage, and tax default. Fines were imposed for damages:

> If a man cut down a tree in the garden of another man, he shall pay one-half mina of silver. (10)
>
> If a man rented an ox and damaged its eye, he shall pay one-half of its price. (35)

The desire for children, so basic to the thought of the Old Testament, is inherent in the Lipit-Ishtar code:

> If a man's wife has not borne him children (but) a harlot (from) the public square has borne him children, he shall provide grain, oil, and clothing for that harlot; the children which the harlot has borne him shall be his heirs, and as long as his wife lives the harlot shall not live in the house with his wife. (27)
>
> If a man married a wife (and) she bore him children and those children are living, and a slave also bore children for her master (but) the father granted freedom to the slave and her children, the children of the slave shall not divide the estate with the children of their (former) master. (25)

Although the Bible never condones consorting with an harlot, it does mention the fact that both Abraham and Jacob had children by female servants in the household. The Nuzi tablets tell us that a barren wife was actually required to provide an handmaid for her husband in order that he might have children. Abraham appears to have given Hagar her freedom after the birth of Isaac (Gen. 21:14), and Scripture makes it clear that Ishmael, her son, did not divide the estate with Isaac, Abraham's son by Sarah (Gen. 17:19-21).

A further provision in the Lipit-Ishtar code states:

> If a man has turned away from his first wife... (but) she has not gone out of his (house), his wife which he married *as his favorite* is a second wife, he shall continue to support his first wife.

Leah, the first wife of Jacob, took a second place in his affections. There was never any thought, however, that she should be divorced in favor of the beloved Rachel. In fact the twelve "children of Israel" (Jacob) had four mothers, Leah, Rachel, and their two handmaids, Bilhah and Zilpah.

Lipit-Ishtar closes his law code with a blessing on those who will not damage the stele on which it was written, and a curse on any who would presume to harm it.

4. Hammurabi

The second year of the reign of the Amorite king of Babylon, Hammurabi, was given the name, "the year when he established justice." Hammurabi built upon the work of his predecessors, but his code is the fullest and best known.

The laws of Hammurabi were inscribed on a black diorite stele, six feet in height, which is now in the Louvre. The stele was discovered by the French archaeologist, Jacques de Morgan, during excavations at the Persian city of Susa (Biblical Shushan) in 1901. Elamites are thought to have taken the stele during one of their many raids on ancient Babylonia.

At the top of the stele is a bas-relief showing Hammurabi standing before the Semitic sun-god, Shamash who, because he encircles the crest of heaven, is also the god of law and justice. The god is depicted with a ring and staff, symbols of royalty, in his right hand. Before him stands Hammurabi, ready to receive the royal authority which will enable him to transmit the laws to his people.

The text of the code, written in Akkadian cuneiform, is written in fifty-one columns on the stele. In its prologue, written in poetry, Hammurabi claims to have been chosen by the gods to bring justice to the land. The poetic epilogue reaffirms the desire of Hammurabi to prevent the strong from oppressing the weak and to protect the interests of the orphan and the widow. Hammurabi directed that the stele be set up in a public place so that his subjects would know their rights.

The laws themselves exhibit a social structure with three classes: an upper class of free-born nobles, an intermediate class of plebeians or commoners, and the lowest class made up of slaves. Priests, merchants, and soldiers were found among the two upper classes. Even slaves, however, had rights which had to be respected, although penalties to those who had wronged them were not as severe as for the upper classes. A monetary value was assigned to slaves; some of whom, however, were free to engage in business. A noble was equal in value to two commoners, and a commoner to two slaves, in the eyes of the law.

These distinctions made in Hammurabi's Code may be contrasted with the Biblical attitude toward various levels of society. Slavery existed in ancient Israel, but it was not a normal part of the social structure and provision was made whereby the Hebrew slave was set free at the sabbatical year (Exod. 21:1-6). Of particular interest is the Biblical attitude toward "strangers" in Israel. The covenant sign of circumcision was given not only to the physical sons of Abraham, but extended to all:

> ...whether born in your house or bought with your money from any foreigner who is not your offspring, both he that is born in your house and he that is bought with your money, shall be circumcised (Gen. 17:12-13).

When it is remembered that Abraham was able to gather a personal army of three hundred and eighteen trained men, "born in his house" to rescue his nephew Lot (Gen. 14:14), we gain a fresh appreciation of the part that non-Israelites played in the patriarchal history.

At the time of the Exodus we read of a "mixed multitude" (Exod. 12:38; Num. 11:4; Josh. 8:35) which accompanied the Israelites. No certain identification can be given to this group, but they appear to have included the children of marriages between Israelites and Egyptians and various groups of non-Israelites who chose to associate themselves with the covenant people.

The time of bondage in Egypt was never forgotten by Israel, and the responsibility for kind treatment of strangers was frequently reinforced by the reminder that Israel had been "strangers in Egypt" (cf. Exod. 23:9; Lev. 19:34). The sympathetic attitude toward strangers is illustrated by the law of the sabbath which specifically mentions them as exempt from work, along with the Israelites (Exod. 20:10).

An important principle of Israelite law states: "Ye shall have one manner of law, as well for the stranger as for the home-born" (Lev. 24:22). This involved responsibility as well as privilege: "He that blasphemeth the name of the Lord, he shall surely be put to death, all the congregation shall certainly stone him, as well the stranger as the home born" (Lev. 24:16).

The Hammurabi law code was purely civil in application. Although mention is made of religious functionaries, and the law itself is traced to the appointment of Hammurabi by the gods, the code itself pertains entirely to the regulation of human conduct on the ethical plane. Conversely the Mosaic law has both moral and religious (ceremonial) aspects as well as those of a strictly civil nature. Comparisons between the Biblical and the Hammurabi code can be made on the level of the regulations which both impress on society. Only the Israelite code has a specific religious motivation.

Even at the level of human relationships, there are great differences between the Israelite code and that of Hammurabi's

Babylon. Until the time of David, Israel was primarily an agricultural people. She was, in fact, less advanced technologically than her neighbors. The Philistines had a monopoly on iron as late as the time of Saul (I Sam. 13:19-22). Babylon, however, was a land with important commercial ventures. A system of canals, connecting the Tigris and the Euphrates Rivers, required the co-operation of many people if the land was to be properly irrigated. All this found expression in the Code of Hammurabi. Even the veterans from the Babylonian wars were granted a kind of "G.I. Bill of Rights."

There are, of course, significant areas of life which the Babylonians shared with the Biblical Hebrews, and numerous places where the two laws overlap. The Biblical principle

> life for life, eye for eye, tooth for tooth, hand for hand, burning for burning, wound for wound, stripe for stripe (Exod. 21:23-25).

is basic in the Hammurabi code. This is spelled out in such detail that a builder who builds a house which collapses and kills the son of the owner of the house is made to suffer by having one of his own sons killed! If a slave is killed under similar circumstances it is enough for the builder to provide another slave of equal value.

According to Deuteronomy 19:18-19, a false witness was to be punished with the penalty he intended to bring upon the other man. In similar vein the Code of Hammurabi states:

> If a (man) came forward with false testimony in a case and has not proved the word which he spoke, if that case was a case involving life, that man shall be put to death. (3)

Several points of parallel may be observed between Babylonian and Israelite law as it pertains to marriage and divorce. In both codes adultery was punishable by death for both parties (Lev. 20:10; Deut. 22:22; Code of Hammurabi, 129).

A woman whose chastity was suspected could have a trial by ordeal according to both the Biblical and the Hammurabi codes, although the nature of the ordeal differed. The Babylonian code (132) provided that the wife who was suspect should be cast into the river which acted as the judge, a method which was earlier mentioned in the Ur-nammu Code. In Numbers 5:11-28 a different ordeal is prescribed. There the priest gives to the woman water in which dust from the sanctuary has been placed and the woman is counted innocent if she does not swell up and die.

Although there is no parallel in Israelite law, the provisions of the Code of Hammurabi whereby a maid servant may be provided by a barren wife so that her husband may have children is illustrated by Sarah's suggestion that Abraham have children by Hagar (Gen. 16:3). The wife is protected by the provision that the slave who bears children does not gain equality with her mistress, and the slave is protected in that she cannot be sold after giving birth to a child of her master (paragraphs 144-147).

Not only were men, under certain circumstances, permitted to divorce their wives, but the aggrieved wife could divorce her husband according to the Babylonian laws (paragraphs 138-141). In the Biblical record mention is only made of the husband divorcing his wife (Deut. 24:1-4).

Proper respect for parents was insisted on in both codes. The Code of Hammurabi reads:

> If a man has struck his father, one shall cut off his hands. (195)

In this instance the Biblical penalty is even more severe:

> He that smiteth his father or his mother shall be surely put to death (Exod. 21:15).

Kidnapping brought the death penalty:

> If a man has stolen the young son of a freeman, he shall be put to death. (14)
>
> He that stealeth a man, or if he be found in his hand, he shall surely be put to death (Exod. 21:16).

Assault on a pregnant woman was considered a heinous crime both in the Code of Hammurabi and the Bible:

> If a man has struck the daughter of a person of the upper class and caused her to drop what is in her womb . . . if that woman has died, one shall put to death his daughter. (209-10)
>
> If men strive, and hurt a woman with child, so that her fruit depart from her, and yet no mischief follow: he shall be surely punished . . . and if any mischief follow, then thou shalt give life for life (Exod. 21:22).

We have seen that the problem of the goring ox had been met as early as the Eshnunna code. The Code of Hammurabi has a similar provision:

> If a (man's) ox was a gorer and his city council made it known to him that it was a gorer, but he did not pad its horns (or) tie up his ox, and that ox gored to death a member of the aristocracy, he shall give one-half mina of silver (251)

Under similar circumstances the Biblical law states:

> If an ox gore a man or a woman that they die: then the ox shall be surely stoned, and his flesh shall not be eaten; but the owner of the ox shall be quit. But if the ox were wont to push with his horn in time past, and it hath been testified to his owner, and he hath not kept him in, but that he hath killed a man or woman; the ox shall be stoned and his owner also shall be put to death (Exod. 21:28-29).

5. The Hittite Code

Our knowledge of Hittite law comes from texts discovered at Boghazkoy, the ancient Hittite capital in Asia Minor. Although dated during the fourteenth century B.C., there can be no doubt that the legal tradition embodied in the code goes back centuries before that time.

Two tablets of a series of Hittite laws have been preserved, and it is known that there was at least one other tablet. The formula "if anyone" is used in introducing each paragraph.

We may infer from the Hittite code that blood revenge was not practiced among the Hittites as it was among the Semites. We read:

> If anyone kills a man or a woman in a quarrel, he has to make amends for him/her. He shall give four persons, man or woman, and pledge his estate for security. (1)

The Hittites did not use the *lex talionis* ("an eye for an eye"), for we are told:

> If anyone blinds a free man or knocks out his teeth, he shall give twenty shekels of silver and pledge his estate as security. (7)

Both blood revenge and the *lex talionis* were marks of a patriarchal society, such as that of the fathers of Israel. With the development of the institutions of government, they tend to be replaced by judicial processes.

Hittites are known to have been in Canaan during patriarchal times, and it is of interest to note that certain principles of Hittite law were observed there. One such provision states:

> If in a village anyone holds fields under socage as inheritance — if the fields have all been given to him, he shall render the services; if the fields have been given to him only to a small part, he shall not render the services. They shall render them from his father's house. (46)

Grants of land were made under Hittite law on condition that the user perform certain military services to the state. When Abraham sought to purchase a burial plot for Sarah in the corner of a field belonging to Ephron, the Hittite (Gen. 23:4), Ephron insisted that he purchase the entire field (Gen. 23:11). Had Abraham purchased only a small part of the field, Ephron would still have had to meet his feudal obligations. By selling the entire field, the obligation passed to Abraham.

The principle of levirate marriage (cf. Deut. 25:5-10) is also reflected in the Hittite law:

> If a man has a wife, and the man dies, his brother shall take his wife, then his father shall take her. If in turn also his father dies, one of his brother's sons shall take the wife whom he had. There shall be no punishment. (193)

This actually goes farther than the Israelite law, for the Hittites made provision for the father of the deceased to take the widow, after the brother. Tamar, in seeking a child by Judah (Gen. 38:12-19), was acting in accord with this principle.

The Biblical patriarchs lived before the codification of Israelite law. Theirs was not a lawless society, however. Our earliest law code, that of Ur-nammu, certainly antedates Abraham. Other codes from Sumer, Babylon, Assyria, and the Hittite lands reflect a legal tradition which bears witness to a highly developed civilization. Certain of the elements of these earlier codes were adapted to the requirements of Israel, and others were repudiated. The patriarchs did not live in a legal vacuum, and an examination of the laws of their neighbors throws much light on their own lives.

17

THE LITERATURE OF THE PATRIARCHAL AGE

We have no records of any written documents among the Israelites prior to the time of Moses. There was a time when men questioned whether the art of writing existed as long ago as the time of Moses (mid-second millennium B.C.). For centuries we thought of ancient history as beginning with Greece. With the discovery of advanced cultures dating back almost two millennia before Moses, doubts concerning the writing ability of the Hebrew lawgiver have been removed.

Another question impresses itself upon us, however. Was there any Israelite literature in the pre-Mosaic era. How did Abraham and his sons pass on to their children the rudiments of their faith?

In some respects the questions are unanswerable. We would suspect that some form of communication existed. Other cultures had developed epic literature which embodied the traditions of the earliest days of the tribe or nation. Since Israel was a part of the environment of the ancient Near East, it probably followed patterns similar to those which are known to have existed in the Tigris-Euphrates valley and at Ugarit.

We are not left entirely to conjecture, however. The reader of the Old Testament is soon aware that the Bible does not contain all of the ancient literature of Israel. In Numbers 21:14 we find a poetic quotation from a book bearing the name, *The Book of the Wars of the Lord*. In Joshua 10:13 and again in II Samuel 1:17, 18, reference is made to a *Book of Jasher,* (or *Book of the Upright*).

All that we actually know about these books is contained in the Scriptures that mention them. A fraudulent *Book of Jasher* which has been published in recent years was probably written about A.D. 1750. E. J. Goodspeed in his small volume entitled

Modern Apocrypha exposes the volume sold as *The Book of Jasher* as one of sixteen famous "Biblical" hoaxes.

The fact that the Biblical quotations from both the *Book of Jasher* and the *Book of the Wars of the Lord* are all poetic in nature leads us to examine other poetry in the Old Testament historical books to determine whether or not the Biblical writers quote from other poetic works.

Semitic poetry is characterized by a structure known as parallelism. In one form of parallelism, a statement is made in one line and the same idea is repeated in other words in the next. Such a pattern occurs in Genesis 4:23-24:

> Adah and Zillah, hear my voices;
> You wives of Lamech, hearken to what I say:
> I have slain a man for wounding me,
> a young man for striking me.
> If Cain is avenged sevenfold,
> truly Lamech seventy-seven fold.

This boastful "Song of Lamech" is an excellent example of Semitic poetry. Adah and Zillah mentioned in the first line form a parallel to "you wives of Lamech" of line two. "Hear" and "hearken" are also synonymous.

There are many other bits of poetry in the book of Genesis. Jacob's blessing of his sons (Gen. 49:2-27) is probably the longest. They each possess the parallelism which particularly attracted the Semites of the ancient Near East. Poets from Assyria and Babylonia, and even non-Semitic Egypt, regularly used this means of expression.

Before the ability to read and write became prevalent there was a strong motivation to produce national and religious literature in poetic form. Poetry can be memorized more readily than prose, and there is evidence that the Greek Iliad and Odyssey were memorized and recited by ancient bards long before Homer reduced them to writing. The Sumerian and Babylonian accounts of the flood are in poetic form, and without doubt had a similar history.

The Biblical doctrine of inspiration defines the end product — the records contained in Scripture — as inspired of God. It does not preclude the use of source material. The later historical books of the Old Testament quote a large number of records which were used by inspired writers — "Chronicles of the Kings of Israel" (I Kings 14:19), "The History of Nathan the Prophet," "The Prophecy of Ahijah the Shilonite," and "The Visions of Iddo the Seer" (II Chron. 10:29).

The Biblical statement that Moses went to school in Egypt (Acts 7:22) implies that the Israelite lawgiver had a wealth of information at his disposal. During the years when he was being raised by his devout mother, Moses certainly was told about the great acts of God in Israel's past. He must have heard about the call of Abraham, the birth of Isaac, the journeyings of Jacob and the descent into Egypt of the tribes while Joseph was Prime Minister. Both at his mother's knee and in the schools of Egypt Moses was prepared for his great work.

Recent scholarship has come to appreciate the accuracy with which oral tradition was transmitted before writing became commonplace. In modern life we do not need to depend upon memory because we can record all information which we deem vital. The multiplicity of our daily reading may actually hinder the process of memory. The Brahmins of India, however, in a culture which is totally different from ours, memorize the 153,826 words of their holy book, the Rigveda. We need not think of the materials of the book of Genesis as passed on in a unit in the age of the patriarchs, but we have every reason to believe that the patriarchs passed on the traditions which they received, and that these, later, under the guidance of the Holy Spirit, were incorporated into our Bible as the Book of Genesis.

BIBLIOGRAPHY

PRIMARY SOURCE MATERIAL

Translations of the Lipit Ishtar, Eshnunna, Hammurabi, Hittite and Assyrian Law Codes, the Ugaritic Epics, the Egyptian Sinuhe Story, selections from Mari and Amarna Letters and Nuzi Legal Documents are readily available in: J. B. Pritchard, ed., *Ancient Near Eastern Texts Relating to the Old Testament* (Princeton, 1955).

Translations of the Code of Hammurabi, the Ugaritic Epics and a selection of Amarna letters will be found in: D. Winston Thomas, ed., *Documents from Old Testament Times* (London: Thomas Nelson, 1958).

Illustrations of the dress, daily life, and religious practices of the Old Testament world are conveniently classified in: J. B. Pritchard, ed., *The Ancient Near East in Pictures Relating to the Old Testament.* (Princeton, 1954).

Translations of the Amarna Letters:

S. A. B. Mercer, *The Tell El-Amarna Tablets* (Toronto, 1939).

J. A. Knudtzon, *Die El-Amarna Tafeln* (Leipzig, 1907-15). Knudtzon's work (in German) is preferred by careful scholars to that of Mercer (in English).

Translation of the Mari Letters:

G. Dossin, Charles F. Jean, and J. R. Kupper, *Archives Royales de Mari* (Paris 1950-). This definitive series of translations is in French.

Translations of the Ugaritic Texts:

G. R. Driver, *Canaanite Myths and Legends* (Edinburgh, 1956).

C. H. Gordon, *Ugaritic Literature* (Rome, 1949).

A popular translation of the three Epics, frequently in the form of paraphrase, is in: Theodor Gaster, *The Oldest Stories in the World* (New York, 1952).

SPECIAL STUDIES

Albrecht Alt, *Der Gott der Vater* (Leipzig, 1929).

C. H. Gordon, "Biblical Customs and the Nuzu Tablets," *The Biblical Archaeologist,* Vol. III, No. 1 (Feb. 1940).

Moshe Greenberg, *The Hab/piru* (American Oriental Series, Volume 39, New Haven, 1955).

Manfred R. Lehman, "Abraham's Purchase of Machpelah and Hittite Law," *Bulletin of the American Schools of Oriental Research,* No. 129 (Feb. 1953).

G. E. Mendenhall, *Law and Covenant in Israel and in the Ancient Near East* (Pittsburgh: The Biblical Colloquium, 1955).

SUGGESTIONS FOR FURTHER READING

Archaeology

Albright, W. F., *Archaeology and the Religion of Israel* (Johns Hopkins, 1942).

———, *The Archaeology of Palestine* (Penguin, 1954).

———, *From the Stone Age to Christianity* (Johns Hopkins, 1946).

Barton, G. A., *Archaeology and the Bible* (American Sunday School Union, 1937).

Burrows, M., *What Mean These Stones?* (Yale, 1941).

Ceram, C. W., *Gods, Graves and Scholars* (Albert A. Knopf, 1954).

———, *The Secret of the Hittites* (Albert A. Knopf, 1956).

Chiera, E., *They Wrote on Clay* (University of Chicago, 1938).

Finegan, J., *Light from the Ancient Past* (Princeton University Press, 1959).

Glueck, N., *The Other Side of the Jordan* (American Schools of Oriental Research, 1940).
Rivers in the Desert (Farrar, Straus, and Cudahy, 1959).

Gordon, C. H., *Adventures in the Nearest East* (Phoenix, 1957).

Rowley, H. H., *Recent Discovery and the Patriarchal Age* (Oxford, 1949).

Kramer, S. N., *From the Tablets of Sumer* (Falcon's Wing Press, 1956).

McCown, C. C., *The Ladder of Progress in Palestine* (Harper, 1943).

———, *Man, Morals, and History* (Harper, 1958).

Pattai, Raphael, *Sex and Family in the Bible* (Doubleday, 1959).

Pritchard, James B., *Archaeology and the Old Testament* (Princeton, 1958).

Rowley, H. H., *Recent Discovery and the Patriarchal Age* (Oxford, 1949).

Unger, M. F., *Archaeology and the Old Testament* (Zondervan, 1954).

Woolley, C. L., *The Sumerians* (Clarendon Press, 1929).

———, *Ur of the Chaldees* (Penguin, 1950).

Wright, G. E., *Biblical Archaeology* (Westminster, 1957).

History

Albright, W. F., "The Biblical Period," *The Jews: Their History, Culture, and Religion.* Louis Finkelstein, ed. (Harper, 1949).

Anderson, B. W., *Understanding the Old Testament* (Prentice-Hall, 1957).

Breasted, James Henry, *A History of Egypt* (Scribner).

Bright, J., *A History of Israel* (Westminster, 1959).

Gordon, C. H., *The World of the Old Testament* (Doubleday, 1958).

Hall, H. R. H., *The Ancient History of the Near East* (Methuen, 1950).

Heinisch, P., tr., Heidt, W., *History of the Old Testament* (Ecclesiastical Press, 1952).

Hill, Dorothy B., *Abraham: His Heritage and Ours* (Beacon Press, 1957).

Lods, A., *Israel* (Kegan, Paul, Trubner and Co., 1932).

Moscati, S., *Ancient Semitic Civilizations* (Elek Books, 1957).

———, *The Face of the Ancient Orient* (Routledge and Kegan Paul, 1960).

Noth, Martin, *The History of Israel* (Harper, 1958).

Oesterley, W.O.E. and Robinson, Theodore, *A History of Israel* (Oxford, 1932).

Pedersen, J., *Israel* (Branner, 1940).

Pieters, A., *Notes on Old Testament History* (Eerdmans, 1950).

Schwartz, Leo, ed., *Great Ages and Ideas of the Jewish People* (Random House, 1956).

Old Testament Theology

Baab, Otto, *The Theology of the Old Testament* (Abingdon-Cokesbury, 1949).

Heinisch, Paul, *Theology of the Old Testament,* tr. William G. Heidt (Liturgical Press, 1955).

Jacob, E., *Theology of the Old Testament* (Hodder and Stoughton, 1958).

Knight, George A. F., *A Christian Theology of the Old Testament* (John Knox Press, 1959).

Koehler, Ludwig, *Old Testament Theology* (Westminster, 1957).

Oehler, Gustav Frederich, *Theology of the Old Testament,* tr. George E. Day (Funk and Wagnalls 1883).

Rowley, H. H., *The Faith of Israel* (S.C.M. Press, 1956).

Smith, J. W. D., *God and Man in Early Israel* (Methuen and Co., 1956).

Snaith, Norman H., *The Distinctive Ideas of the Old Testament* (Epworth Press, 1944).

Vos, Geerhardus, *Biblical Theology* (Eerdmans, 1948).

Vriezen, T. C., *An Outline of Old Testament Theology* (Black, 1958).

Wright, G. E., "The Faith of Israel," (*The Interpreter's Bible,* Vol. 1, Nashville, 1952).

———, *The God Who Acts* (S.C.M. Press, 1952).

INDEX

Abam-ram, 31
Abel, 92
Abiezer, 87
Abimelech, 90
Abraham, 13, 15, 16, 19, 20, 21, 23, 24, 29, 31, 35, 38, 44, 45, 47, 57, 59, 71, 74, 77, 86, 87, 89, 90, 91, 92, 94, 97, 99, 100, 102, 103, 104, 105, 112, 116, 119
Adah, 66
Admah, 59
Adonis, 68, 69
Adrammelech, 67
Agriculture, 73
Ahaz, 67, 68
Ahijah, 87, 118
Aijalon, 66
Akkadian, 30, 31, 33, 108, 111
Albright, W. F., 11, 12, 47, 50, 51, 55, 85
Alt, Albrecht, 85
Amenemhet, 51
Ammon, 67
Ammonites, 94
Amon Re, 38
Amorites, 19, 31, 32, 40, 49, 50, 61, 63, 111
Amosis, 40, 41
Amraphel, 57
Anammelech, 67
Anat, 64
Angels, 98
Angel of the Lord, 105
Antart, 64
Aphaea, 69
Aphek, 35
Aqabah, Gulf of, 58
Arabian Desert, 54
Arabs, 31, 61, 103
Aram, 31
Aramaeans, 31, 45
Aram-naharaim, 45
Arioch, 57
Arriwuk, 57
Arvadites, 19
Ashdod, 66
Asherah, 62, 65
Asherat, 62
Ashteroth-karnaim, 58
Ashtoreth, 68
Asiatics, 52
Assyria, 33
Astarte, 65, 68
Avaris, 40

Baal, 61, 62, 63, 86, 93
Baal-gad, 64
Baal-hazor, 64
Baal-zebul, 64
Baal-zephon, 64
Babylonia, 32, 113, 116
Babylonians, 31, 101
Balaam, 63
Balak, 63
Balikh River, 45
Beel-zebul, 64
Beer-sheba, 11, 20, 93
Beni Hasan, 38, 41, 74
Benjamin, 15, 27, 71
Benjaminites, 31
Bethel, 27, 47, 91
Beth-horon, 66
Beth-shan, 66
Beth-shemesh, 65
Beth-yerah, 65
Betrothal, 82
Bilalama, 108, 109
Bilhah, 78, 110
Boghazkoy, 80, 115
Brahmins, 119
Bread, 74
Breasted, J. H., 29, 36
Bright, John, 13
Bromiley, G. W., 105
Bronze, 39
Byblos, 32, 52, 68, 69

Cadmus, 56
Cain, 92
Campbell, Edward F., 46
Canaan, 19, 21, 23, 43, 49, 50, 51, 52, 53, 54, 69, 80, 82, 91, 98, 99, 100
Canaanites, 20, 31, 35, 40, 50, 55, 61, 68
Carchemish, 32
Carmel, 50
Carthage, 68
Chariots, 40
Chastity, 113

Chedorlaomer, 57, 58
Cheops, 37
Chephren, 37
Children, 110
Cinyras, 68
Circumcision, 20, 94, 95, 112
Cossaeans, 33
Crete, 32, 61
Curds, 73
Cyprus, 32, 61

Dagan, 66
Dagon, 66
Damascus, 45, 58, 59
Dan, 58
Danell, G.A., 11
David, 101, 113
Davis, John, 67
Day of Atonement, 92
DeMorgan, J., 111
Dinah, 26, 93
Djoser, 37
Dothan, 73
Dress, 74
Dumuzi, 69

Edom(ites), 25, 94, 101, 115
Egypt(ians), 20, 23, 25, 35, 36, 53, 94, 99, 100, 112, 119
Ekron, 64, 100
El, 62
Elam(ites), 44, 57, 71
Elat, 62
El-Bethel, 93
El-Elyon, 86
Eliezer, 77
Elijah, 68
Ellasar, 57
Eloquent Peasant, 39
El-paran, 58
Emim, 58
En Mishpat, 58
En Shemesh, 65
Ensi, 29, 30
Ephraim, 27
Ephron, 16, 53, 80, 115
Er, 82
Erech, 29
Esau, 17, 20, 24, 25, 26, 46, 79, 91, 98, 101
Esdraelon, 50, 54
Esh-baal, 64
Eshnunna, 81, 108, 109, 114
Euphrates, 41, 113

Faiyum, 39
Family, 17
First Intermediate Period, 38
Flood, 43
Form Criticism, 12, 13

Garstang, John, 54
Gaster, Theodore H., 65, 66
Gaza, 66
Gerar, 47, 73, 92
Gezer, 50, 55
Gibeonites, 79
Gideon, 17
Gilboa, 66
Girgashites, 50
Glueck, Nelson, 51, 58
Goetze, Albrecht, 108
Gomorrah, 51, 98
Goodspeed, E. J., 117
Gordon, Cyrus H., 69, 71

Hagar, 24, 52, 71, 72, 78, 104, 110, 114
Hall, H. R., 43
Ham, 36
Hamathites, 19
Hammurabi, 15, 33, 44, 78, 107, 108, 111, 112, 113, 114
Hannibal, 68
Hapiru, 34, 35, 36
Haran, 23, 26, 31, 43, 44, 45, 65, 77
Harp, 75
Harper, Song of, 39
Hazezon-tamar, 58
Hebrew, 35
Hebron, 11, 46, 73
Hephaestus, 66
Herodotus, 37
Hieroglyphic, 36
Hinnom, Valley of, 67
Hittite Law Code, 83, 115
Hittites, 20, 25, 34, 50, 71, 82, 83, 116
Hivites, 50
Hobab, 20
Hobah, 59
Honey, 73
Horites (Hurrians), 33, 50
Horon, 66
Hurrians, 33, 34
Hyksos, 38, 40, 41, 46

Ibshe, 38
Imhotep, 37
Indo-Aryan, 33, 34
Isaac, 11, 13, 16, 20, 24, 25, 29, 40, 73, 89, 97, 100
Ishbi-irra, 44

Ishbosheth, 64
Ishmael, 72, 78, 90, 99, 100, 101, 104
Isin, 32, 33, 44, 109
Israel, 11, 17, 35

Jabbok, 26, 91
Jacob, 13, 15, 16, 20, 21, 24, 25, 26, 27, 29, 46, 53, 62, 78, 79, 83, 93, 100, 105, 119
Jacob-el, 31
James, 24
Jasher, Book of, 117, 118
Jebusites, 19
Jeremiah, 67
Jericho, 50, 54, 55
Jerusalem, 69, 101
Jesus, 101
Jezebel, 68
Jonah, 35
Jonathan, 64, 66
Joseph, 15, 20, 27, 29, 35, 53, 98, 99, 100
Josephus, Flavius, 40, 68
Joshua, 36
Josiah, 67
Jubal, 66
Judah, 16, 17, 20, 82, 98, 100, 101, 116
Judgment, 98

Kadesh, 58
Kamose, 40
Kantara, 53
Karatepe, 66
Karnak, 38
Kassites, 33
Kauthar, 66
Kedem, 52, 56
Kedeshim, *Kedeshoth*, 63
Keturah, 19
Khafre, 37
Khnumhotep, 38
Khufu, 37
King List, 43, 44
Koshar, 66
Kramer, Samuel N., 109
Kudur-mabuk, 57

Laban, 26, 46, 72, 79, 83, 85, 92
Lagash, 29, 30
Lamech, 66
Lamech, Song of, 118
Larsa, 33, 44, 57, 58
Law, 17, 93
Leah, 55, 72, 78, 81, 83, 110
Lebanon, 68
Lehman, Manfred R., 80
Lex Talionis, 115
Levi, 93
Leviathan, 66, 67
Levirate marriage, 81, 82, 115
Lipit-Ishtar, 32, 109, 110
Lods, Adolphe, 93
Lot, 16, 20, 24, 51, 57, 58, 59, 90, 98, 112
Lotan, 66
Lower Egypt, 38
Lugal, 30
Lulubi, 30
Luz, 47
Lyre, 75

Macalister, R. A. S., 55
Malach-baal, 67
Malik, 67
Mamre, 47
Manasseh, 17, 27, 67
Mandrakes, 55
Mari, 12, 13, 31, 32, 33, 57, 67
Marriage, 83
Maryannu, 34
Mastaba, 37
Mazzebah, 63
Megiddo, 50
Melchizedek, 85, 86
Melkarth, 67
Memphis, 38
Mendenhall, George, 86
Mephibosheth, 64
Merib-baal, 64
Mes-anni-padda, 44
Mesopotamia, 103
Middle Assyrian Law Code, 83
Middle Kingdom, 39
Midian(ite), 17, 19, 20, 63
Milch-baal, 67
Milcom, 67
Mishor, 65
Mitanni, 33, 34
Mizpah, 92
Mizraim, 36
Moabites, 94
Mohar, 80
Molech, 67, 68
Moriah, 15, 24, 93, 99, 104
Mosaic Law, 83, 94, 99, 112
Moses, 20, 35, 117
Mot, 64, 66, 69
Muilenberg, J., 13
Muluk, 67

Nabonidus, 43, 44
Nanna, 44, 85, 108

Naram-sin, 30
Nathan, 118
Negev, 43, 46
Nile River, 37, 54
Nineveh, 33, 45
Nin-gal, 44
Nippur, 109
Noah, 92
Nubia, 37, 38, 41
Nuzi, 12, 13, 33, 55, 77, 78, 79, 81, 110

Obadiah, 101
On, 20
Onan, 82
Oxen, 109, 114

Paddan-aram, 19, 20, 29, 31, 45, 72, 77, 80, 89, 91, 92, 105
Palmyrenes, 67
Parity treaty, 86
Parrot, André, 32
Patriarch, 15
Paul, 24, 100, 101
Pedersen, J., 11
Peleg, 31
Peniel, 26
Peor, 63
Petrie, Sir Flinders, 47
Phaliga, 31
Pharaoh, 23, 35, 36, 97, 99
Philistines, 35, 71, 113
Philo of Byblos, 65, 66
Phoenicians, 49, 54, 56, 68
Pieters, Albertus, 68
Potiphar, 35, 99
Potiphera, 20
Prayer, 89, 90, 91
Promises, 100
Ptah, 66
Punt, 37
Pyramid Age, 38
Pyramids, 37

Rachel, 26, 27, 46, 78, 79, 80, 81, 83, 110
Rahab, 20
Ramesses II, 36
Ras Shamra (Ugarit), 49, 61
Rebekah, 20, 24, 25, 72, 81, 91
Rehoboth, 25
Rephaim, 58
Resheph, 66
Retjenu, 52
Reuben, 15, 17
Rigveda, 119
Rim-sin, 44
Rubuti, 46
Ruth, 20

Sabbatical Year, 111
Sacrifices, 89, 92, 93
Salitis, 40
Samson, 83
Samsu-iluna, 33, 44
Saqqara, 37
Sarah, 23, 24, 72, 78, 90, 97, 104
Sarai, 104
Sargon of Akkad, 30, 44
Sarugi, 31
Saul, 66
Schools, 38
Sedeq, 65
Seele, Keith, 41
Seir, 26
Semitic, 31
Sephorvaim, 67
Serug, 31
Sesostris, 51
Seth, 89
Shahar, 65
Shamash, 65, 111
Shamshi-Adad, 32
Shapash, 65
Sharon, 50
Sharuhen, 40
Shaveh-kiriathaim, 58
Shechem(ite), 26, 46, 51, 71, 73, 93
Shelah, 82
Shinar, 57
Shipwrecked Sailor, 39
Shuah, 19
Shubad, Queen, 44
Shur, 52
Siddim, Valley of, 58
Sidon, 56
Simeon, 15, 71, 93
Sin (the Moon God), 65
Sin, 99
Sinai, 39, 87
Sinites, 19
Sinuhe, 39, 51, 52, 53, 54
Slavery, 111
Smith, George Adam, 49
Sodom, 35, 51, 59, 89, 98, 99, 104
Solomon, 51, 67
Steindorff, G., 41
Stephen, 102
Sumer(ians), 29, 30, 31, 32, 43, 44, 56
Susa, 111
Suzerainty treaty, 86, 87
Syria, 32, 49

Tamar, 16, 82, 116
Tammuz, 69
Tanis, 46
Taylor, J. E., 43
Teleilat el-Ghassul, 50
Tell Balatah, 46
Terah, 31, 43, 45, 85
Teraphim, 16, 79
Thebes, 38
Theophany, 104
Tidal, 57, 58
Tigris, 113
Til-Turakhi, 31
Tishpak, 109
Titimaeus, 40
Tophet, 67
Tribe, 17
Trinity, 105
Tubal-cain, 66
Tudhalias, 58
Tyre, 56, 68

Ugarit, 32, 49, 56, 94, 117
Ur, 23, 24, 29, 43, 44, 45, 61, 65, 71, 87
Ur-nammu, 30, 44, 45, 107, 108, 113, 116
Ura, 71
Urukagina, 30

Von Rad, Gerhard, 12
Vos, Geerhardus, 105
Vulcan, 66

Wages, 109
Wars of the Lord, Book of, 117, 118
Wright, George Ernest, 46

Yam, 66
Yareah, 65
Yasmah-adad, 32

Zagros Mts., 32
Zeboiim, 58
Zemarites, 19
Zillah, 66
Zilpah, 78
Zimri-Lim, 32
Zoan, 46
Zoar, 51
Zuzim, 58